PHENOMENAL
BRAIN POWER

From Brain Injury to Brain Awakening

Mia Dalene Marcum-McCoy, M.A.

foreword by
Fred P. Langer, RN, Esq.

Shancie,
This is the book
Wnk (Rose) Coached me
to finish.

Mia D. Marcum-M°Coy
12 · 14 · 17

Phenomenal Brain Power

From Brain Injury to Brain Awakening

ISBN-13: 978-1505756388
ISBN-10: 1505756383

Cover & Interior Design
By Tony McCoy

All profits from this book go to charity for the purpose of increasing the quality of life for those living with brain injury. To learn more about where funds go and the people you help, visit www.phenomenalbrainpower.com

Acknowledgements

The Moving On rehabilitation class taught by Gail Tumlinson and Craig Sicilia let me see that I am still a whole person after brain injury and that I have a voice and a place in the world. Craig's challenge pulled my brain from the depths of despair and put me on the path of finding solutions. As I got to know my fellow students, I saw patterns in their struggles which eventually led me to discover my mission.

Ulrike Berzau for suggesting that my story was inspirational and should be made into a book.

Donna Kozik's program, Write a Book In a Weekend, provided structure and support while I was writing this book.

Fred Langer for his dedication to people living with brain injury and his encouragement of me in my efforts to inspire others.

To my editors, Tony, Martha, Meredith, Morgan, Darla, George and Lori.

Special thanks to Tony and Martha who sat with me and helped me convey my thoughts into words, and friends and family for their encouragement.

This book is dedicated to Stephen McCloskey,

who told me to make my injury sing.

When people have bad things happen to them in our culture we are conditioned to ask "Why me?" when the reality is that we should be saying "Why *not* me?" As far as I can tell no one is immune to trauma. But life has shown me that it is what you *do* with the injury, the illness, the death, the divorce or any other loss, that is most important. I am living proof of this.

In the matter of just a few years I lost my father, my little brother, followed by my mom and two close aunts. In that same time period, I was diagnosed with cancer for the second time, my dear wife and I suffered through two miscarriages and I had my second serious bicycle accident which required multiple hand surgeries. To top it off, complications from my first cancer have recently left me nearly speechless, literally.

I could go on and on. The point is that we are not supposed to wallow through our challenges alone. Nor are we merely to aim to be a "survivor." Our best option and the one that leads to our *true* healing, as corny as it sounds, is to embrace the trauma and make it *sing* like an opera star for any and all who can hear the message. We can and will *thrive* not just survive life's traumatic events. I say, make your bad stuff sing by sharing your voice with those who need to hear it most on this journey. And remember that opera isn't meant to be sung quietly from the back of the room—but right up there on stage under the lights. Get out there and sing!

– Stephen McCloskey

Foreword

This book was written by Mia Marcum-McCoy, a courageous brain injury survivor. I had the privilege to represent Mia. Phenomenal Brain Power chronicles the struggles of a brain injury survivor regrouping herself to find meaning and a joyful life. It is also a general roadmap for other survivors and their loved ones to show that recovery and a purposeful life can happen after brain injury.

Mia's story is extraordinary because it is both common and unique. Here, the reader will learn about problems common to many brain injury survivors; yet it is unique because Mia met these challenges with optimism and courage. In short, she rediscovered herself. It was my honor to represent Mia and to write this foreword to introduce this important piece for brain injury survivors.

– Fred P. Langer, RN, Esq.

PART ONE

"The real troubles in your life are apt to be things that never crossed your worried mind... The kind that blindsides you at 4 p.m. on some idle Tuesday."

– Baz Luhrmann

Introduction

The car ran the stop sign and plowed into my right side. I was now being hit broadside, *T-boned*. The bumper clipped my right ankle on an upward stroke of the pedal. I felt my bicycle being pulled to the left as it was being pushed out from under me by the car. My body went limp. I bounced off the hood of the pretty blue Honda. My mind registered its distinctive color under me just before the lights went out. Everything went dark from the first head hit on the hood of the car to the last head hit, when the top of my helmeted head connected with the pavement and stopped my trajectory a fair distance from the passenger's side door.

During this brief period I was aware of stillness beyond peace and time that I cannot describe in words. I felt like I was drifting toward something so wonderful and was starting to connect with it. I was making this ominous connection with that something when I was distracted by a noise, and my calm response was, *Oh, it sounds like someone got the wind knocked out of them.* At that moment of putting my attention toward the sound, I realized, *It's me!* At the point of recognition I felt myself slip quickly back into my body and the awareness of being engulfed in physical pain. I observed it first at my toes and followed the burning sensation all the way up to my head. I was aware of this while the stillness in the background, that I was also a part of, continued to calmly observe, *Hmm, that's interesting, it's all the same pain.*

And then I heard a silent voice in panic, *Who will take care of my children if I'm not there?!* I heard my physical voice yelling and crying out. First in despair at the thought of my children being left without me, and then my attention went to the physical pain. I cried out in reaction to the tremendous physical agony, followed by the realization I was going to be late for work. Anger welled up inside me toward those that were making me late. By now the annoying ones that hit me had jumped out of their car to make sure I was okay. They were holding me down to the pavement in an attempt to keep me still. The thought drifted in, *Where's my right shoe?*

I could hear sirens approaching. I was coming back to my senses and I was mad as hell. I demanded a cell phone to call my work to tell them I was going to be late. I didn't know how long this was going to take. My words were indistinguishable to the woman trying to make the phone call for me. I grabbed the phone from her hand and dialed it myself. It took two tries for me to get the numbers right. I announced my dilemma to the company operator and instructed her to deliver the message immediately to my boss. Now I was *fuming* as the reality of the situation sunk in. I was actually going to be late to work! I screamed to the sky, "Get these people away from me!" I began flailing my arms to bat the perpetrators away. I struggled to escape. My brain was buzzing, swirling, confused.

Chapter One

I was a single mother of two rambunctious children, ages six and nine. I was intelligent, highly educated, and making strides at rebuilding my life after the dissolution of a 10-year marriage. Riding my bicycle to work was my strategy for moving past the feelings of anger and disappointment while getting a great workout on a busy single mom's schedule. The ride in made me calm and focused and I arrived refreshed and ready for challenge. My vision of life included working until the day I died, somewhere into my 70s.

I couldn't imagine my life without working and earning an income. I felt powerful and free when I strategized investing the money I earned. A rush of excitement mixed with financial prowess made me feel a sensation I can only describe as near world domination. It was as if anything was possible. I loved the intellectual stimulation and challenge of a good puzzle. This was echoed in my daily employment with computer software. I was so wrapped up in it all; my children, my job title at the headquarters of a fast paced and fast growing company, and of course, my salary. These things defined me. They announced my worth to the world, at least in my eyes. Until July 2, 2001 when a tragic gift of an accident widened my scope of what is possible in the human experience. *My human experience.*

At the scene of the accident my attempt to get away was successful and I was wandering unknowingly into the street, toward traffic. My backpack hung from my shoulders, my right shoe was missing, and I was holding my bloody left arm. I felt a hand on my right elbow as I heard the firefighter's words, "Hey, where are you going?" a brief chuckle, and then, "Let's sit down over here." I was redirected to the safety of the sidewalk.

The paramedics had arrived and I was put through a series of tests; an obstacle course of words and following commands. My body was full of adrenaline and endorphins and completely numb. My brain continued to swirl. I was coming more into the present moment and going into shock. The paramedic was keeping his eyes on me and searching for signs of difficulty. I was fading in and out. I wanted to close my eyes and drift but my silence was met with a barrage of questions. I was being kept awake and lucid.

Police were assessing the scene. My conversation with the officers was muddy. I couldn't say the car stopped at the sign because I took my eyes off of it when I saw it looked like it was going to stop. I was confused. If the car stopped I should have made it through the intersection, right? The police determined the car was traveling at 20 miles per hour at the time of impact based on where everything landed. The next day at work I would share this with my boss, to which he would look at me in amazement and announce, "A professional boxer takes a punch to the head at ten miles per hour. You took double that to your entire body!" *Perspective.*

I was brought into the emergency room on the mandatory backboard. My body was now writhing in pain and moving on its own. They were trying to keep me still and my body wouldn't have it. It needed to move. I was spotted with bloody road rash and a large gouge of skin was taken out of my left arm. It had stopped bleeding on its own. The attending physician twisted the suspicious looking forearm but when I didn't cry out in pain they informed me they couldn't find anything broken. I was asked where the most pain was and my attention went to my ankles. They felt like they were shattered and I didn't know if I could walk. *CLUE: I had forgotten I was walking at the scene of the accident.*

A series of budget cuts meant the emergency room was saving money, and because I had no outward signs of broken bones and no noticeable holes in my skull no X-rays for fractures nor MRI were taken. Instead the doctor visually inspected my Styrofoam helmet and reported, "No damage here!" I pointed out the deep gouge and another indentation in the back of the helmet that was new. I was instructed to return in three days if the pain persisted. Then they would take X-rays.

I wanted out of the emergency room and to go to work. I was making calls to family and friends to find someone to pick me up but was only reaching answering machines. I begged the attending physician to release me on my own since I couldn't find anyone who could retrieve me. I wanted to get to work. I was late. I was missing my meeting to learn databases. The doctor and I were now in negotiations for my release and he agreed to discharge me on my own under two conditions: one, I had to go directly home and rest; I couldn't go to work. Two, I had to take the vial of pain medication he prescribed.

This was all new to me. To this point in my life I had been relatively pain-free. I hadn't experienced anything more than minor sprains before, not counting childbirth. I argued I didn't need anything stronger than Tylenol. My body was still pumping copious amounts of adrenaline and endorphins; adrenaline was providing the fight-or-flight response while endorphins were numbing me out.

I was released from the emergency room but needed to get to work to unload my backpack and orient myself. It was the first stop on my trek back home. I must have looked pretty rough walking the six blocks to my office with patches of dried, bloody road rash spotting my exposed skin, helmet in hand. A homeless man camped out on the sidewalk looked at me with surprise and concern and asked, "Do you need some help?" *Ironic.*

I hadn't believed the emergency room physician when he warned me I would feel much worse the next day, when the endorphins wore off. He was wrong. It took *two* full days, and on the third day I woke up and couldn't move. I was in such horrendous pain that I was crying when I called into work to tell them I wasn't able to make it in that day.

In Court

Within weeks of the accident I received a subpoena to appear in court. The driver was fighting the ticket he received at the scene of the accident, arguing the damage my body caused to his car showed that I hit *him*. He was suing me for damages to his vehicle and attempting to prove it was my fault. After quietly listening to the argument the judge ruled in my favor because I had the right of way. The driver's failure to stop was duly noted. In the broader scope it didn't matter. The reality was my body and my bicycle were damaged.

Insurance Company

Complete restoration of his vehicle involved replacing the front quarter panel on the driver's side, the hood, and the front bumper. I joked to relieve the pain of my loss: *I didn't know I could make such a big impact!* I silently delighted in the fact that I took out as much of his car as I did. I was angry that he got his car fixed while my bicycle was totaled and the tremendous amount of physical pain had become a permanent fixture in my life.

My bicycle was scrapped for usable parts. The seat, handlebars, and wraps were salvageable. Impact had torqued the frame and mangled the tires into the shape of tacos. My bicycle was written off as old. I received a check in the amount equal to their estimate of the bike's adjusted value on the day of the accident, but the dollars for the damaged goods were not enough for an equivalent replacement. The bike had been priceless to me. As my fight with his insurance company ensued, my education into the world of insurance began. This process provided me a whole new perspective regarding insurance companies as a business and the practices of their representatives.

Chapter Two
The Difficulties

I returned to work the day after the accident eager to continue my dream of working for this company. I had planned to advance into a career of computer programming and looked forward to the promise that lifestyle represented to me and my children's future. To this point my work had been stellar. I had surpassed expectations and excelled at everything the company was throwing my way. It was normal for me to complete projects days and weeks ahead of schedule, and on one occasion an entire month ahead of deadline. I could be counted on.

I learned quickly and found solutions with ease. It was automatic. I would put the situation in my 'brain maze' and out popped several different ways to solve it. I loved solving puzzles. I *loved* my job and this company. It was the best place I had ever worked. My *can-do* attitude was popular and appreciated in the workplace, and my positive disposition fit in well with the company culture.

The big shift was sudden. In those early weeks back at work I struggled with the simplest of tasks while co-workers looked at me in awe for having survived being hit by a car. I became a quasi-celebrity and was followed by jokes and smart quips about me keeping my day job in computers and halting any career ambitions as a stuntwoman.

Before the accident I was the person that skipped every other stair with the goal to jump past three at a time. Once the endorphins wore off, continuous pain engulfed my body and I began making shifts in my daily routine. I started riding the elevator up the three flights to my office. One day I got in the elevator with three cyclists. I marveled at their colorful gear and salivated over their pedal cleats and we created an instant bond.

While we moved three floors towards the heavens I learned each one of them had also been hit by cars. I was the newbie with only one hit. Others had at least two. One guy even shared his five-hit status with a smile and a sense of righteousness for his place sharing the road with motor vehicles and their stupid, unaware drivers. We all looked at him in amazement like religious believers realizing they were looking at the Messiah. "Share the Road" was a popular bumper sticker. It was also this guy's passion. Teaching drivers to share the road and pay attention seemed to be his mission in life.

My experience told me that no matter who has the right of way, the hard body is going to win. Suddenly living with the purpose of being there for my children meant more to me than "sharing the road." My love affair with cycling and feeling the freedom that comes with the breeze on my bare skin had given way to fear and panic and the practicality of physics, trajectory, and the realization that I was mortal. The week before the accident I was immortal, riding within inches of hardbody cars traveling at high speeds as I made my way down the hills of Seattle toward the bike path that led home. During that ride I felt righteous. I felt an ease to riding as I diverted from the opening doors of parked cars, near misses, and drivers honking in protest at my skinny, delicate frame sharing the road with their SUVs.

My new cycling comrades all looked okay and none of them said anything about impaired nervous system function or living with constant pain as a result of their bicycle-versus-automobile mishaps. I was impressed each one of them had gotten back onto their bicycle and rode again. I knew I needed to get back on as well, but I was having episodes of reliving the accident and I was fearful of being on a bicycle.

In the months that followed, I did get back on and even rode to work over the same path I took the day I was hit. It was a major milestone, but I couldn't sustain it as the constant physical pain was being joined by post-traumatic stress disorder (PTSD). I was no longer comfortable seeing bicyclists on the road. The feeling would start in my gut, wrenching in panic as a shortness of breath brought me to near hyperventilation behind my steering wheel. I slowed way down and gave cyclists an overstated wide berth. When I couldn't get around them I slowed to a crawl, staying behind them as if to protect them from the long line of traffic behind me. I started talking through my windshield to the riders with unfastened chin straps and no helmets and would announce,

"Buckle that helmet, it's not a banana!" and "Oh, good lord, put a helmet on!" My children informed me the riders couldn't hear my roadside commentary. It was like I was trying to reach back in time and warn myself of my impending doom, as if those riders were on a path to the same impactful destination I had experienced.

I dismissed my sudden difficulties with a continuous looping playlist of possibilities that included pending menopause, stress, and pain as the primary reasons why my memory could be compromised and why I couldn't focus long enough to complete any task. The reasons came from articles I read in magazines, conversations with friends, and even possibilities offered by my general physician. When my doctor suggested pre-menopause I balked and stated I was only 38! She countered with the likelihood of peri-pre-menopause, but ended her sentence with a tonal lift that suggested a question rather than a real possibility. "Is *that* even real?!" slipped out of my mouth.

Friends and acquaintances I talked to had their own reasons for my slip in functioning. I started hearing people respond to my loss of words and even total mid-sentence derailments in my train of thought as 'senior moments,' although my age didn't qualify me as a senior. This was unreasonable from a scientific standpoint. Their next line of defense would attribute my behavior to stress. They made my slip-ups okay in their minds with the camaraderie of shared experience, and soon I was hearing a lot of, "I do that too!" I became alarmed at the ease with which they passed it off.

I knew enough to understand this wasn't normal for me, and my scientific mind continued to search for the one ultimate truth that would explain everything. I observed people's responses to my slipping mental faculties as their need to make me 'okay.' I believe most people want those around them to be all right, so when slips occur in their loved ones their brains are quick to rationalize with thoughts that make them okay, much like our brains do when filling in the visual blanks of a picture.

Even my landlord chimed in, saying his wife suffered profound memory deficits as a result of thyroid issues. Medication made all the difference for her and he suggested I go get my thyroid checked. I tried on each possibility like Cinderella's stepsisters trying on the glass slipper. Nothing fit. I talked myself through the list when my worry level escalated. The multitude of possibilities ended with me trying to refocus on the task at hand and ignore the swirling sensation in my head. Then it would loop and play again as if it was new information I hadn't considered before. *CLUE: Short-term memory loss. But since no one was monitoring my thoughts no one knew.*

The realities of living a stress-filled life was a popular topic in magazine articles. The articles usually contained a long list of symptoms and stated the wide range of ways even common daily stress can affect people. This was enough evidence to add it to my repertoire of possibilities. Everything I had been going through in the last two years could be contributing to my difficulties in functioning; the divorce and the aftermath, moving, caring for two small children, and starting a new career. The part of my mind that wanted a reasonable answer to this affliction kept busy chewing on this possibility. The 'brain maze' I had previously been using to solve software problems was now in a state of perpetual looping to harmonize my symptoms with a 'normal' life.

The fact that I was in pain from head to toe every moment of every day was placed into perspective when a member of upper management, whom I respected, shared his tragic story of how he broke all the major bones in his body and how he was living with constant pain. Now we were in the same club. His suggestion to not let the pain stop me from doing my job well fit in with my years of athletic training. I was used to the "no pain, no gain" attitude. I persevered. When my attention was caught by the unimaginable physical agony I would redirect my thoughts. I was grateful for my opportunities and I held onto that.

The life of mental agility and skill that I had been living was gone, and although I was not aware of what had happened I was in the process of acclimating to the new life. My brain felt like someone traded out my turbo processor for a Pong game. There had been no memo announcing the abrupt transition, only the trickle revealing itself with every movement, every breath. Every previous strength I had was now in deficit. I was in a slow motion burn, but didn't realize I was on fire.

There was a woman in the company who had sustained a brain injury ten years earlier, but kept it quiet from everyone in fear she would be singled out and fired. She came to the company two years before me, after having worked diligently for eight years to rebuild her mental faculties. Her job here was the reward for all her hard work and efforts. She was moving quickly up in the company as well. She had no residual physical evidence suggesting anything tragic had ever happened to her. No one could tell she had played Sleeping Beauty as she lay in a coma for three months, one decade prior.

She was quiet with a warm smile and wise eyes. She watched me from a distance and spoke to me through one of the co-workers on my software team. Alannah was her close friend and the only person in the company who knew and kept her secret. Looking back, I recognize her sticky note strategy, a visual cue to aid her short-term memory deficit, used to help her stay on task and complete projects on time. Back then I had no idea what brain injury entailed. Now I can spot people with brain injury all around me, and when I do it's with a silent, kindred nod of understanding and appreciation for all they have been through and respect for their strength and sheer will to live another day. But back then I had just started living it out in 3D.

Meanwhile, I couldn't figure out why Alannah kept telling me those damn stories about the crazy behavior of a *woman she knew* that had sustained brain injury. First it was about how she would leave her house without the proper clothing and without realizing what she was doing. I heard the one about how she wore shorts and a T-shirt in a blizzard and thought nothing of it. Then there was the onslaught of stories with the common theme of forgetful escapades, like the one where she got dressed and got on the bus to go to work only to look down and realize she wasn't wearing any shoes.

I was screaming in my head for Alannah to stop with these incessant stories! I was on the verge of letting it out of my mouth if I had to listen to another one about how the woman was locked out of her apartment several times a week. I couldn't see what this had to do with me. Maybe Alannah needed to talk. I chalked it up to annoying co-worker syndrome. I found myself telling her, "I have two children to raise," as I held up my *talk to the hand* sign. "Nothing could be wrong with me!" Deep down I must have known something tragic was going on.

During those early, naïve days filled with pain I decided I would be back to my old self in about three weeks. Instead of the pain lessening, it increased. Maybe it was the constant experience of it that finally got to me. That third week I was sitting in front of my computer and my back seized up. The pain was now beyond unbearable. I was quietly crying in my cubicle working through it as any good employee and any good athlete would. Alannah's fingers appeared atop the cubicle wall holding a sticky note with the name and number of a reputable chiropractor.

I took an early lunch break and made my way to his office. There was no smooth curve to my spine when I tried to bend. X-rays showed three points of injury; one in the lower portion of my mid back, one in my mid back, and one in my neck. The damage revealed in these first x-rays identified a slight leftward movement of vertebrae in my neck at C6 and C7. I was lucky to be moving and walking. Any more movement of the vertebrae in this area and I would be adjusting to life as a quadriplegic instead of pain alerting me to the damage. A year later when I requested the doctor's notes for my legal case, I would read the words, "Prognosis is poor for a full recovery." The damage was permanent.

On the day of the accident, I was scheduled to start working out for a triathlon. The pain stopped any physical momentum toward that goal. A couple of months later I was still feeling pain when the sensation of internal weakness—weak to my core—came to the forefront. I signed myself up for physical therapy thinking it would help me regain some strength and stamina. That didn't go too well. I had days where I didn't know what was wrong with me. My body wasn't doing what I was telling it to do. My energy fluctuated and my body was having difficulty regulating its temperature. I sensed that something was wrong when the internal weak sensation became predominant. It had been several weeks of diligent workouts and I wasn't improving. The physical therapist was concerned and suggested I go to my general physician to get checked out.

When I arrived at the appointment with my general practitioner she listened to me and I watched her smile turn into wide-eyed panic. She began testing me and started with the usual, "Do you know what today's date is?" I didn't know.

"Do you know what day of the week it is?"

I answered correctly.

"Who is the president?"

I named one that hadn't been in office for three terms. Her eyes inspected one side of my face and then the other.

"Do you know what this is?" She held something up. I was lost in silent contemplation searching for the word but there was only space in my brain. I didn't know what it was called but I knew it was my favorite object. The shift in my mental acuity revealed itself in that moment. I began to cry and asked her, "What is wrong with me?!" Her face registered alarm and her eyes darted faster from one side of my face to the other.

"I don't know," she said. "I think you might have had a stroke." She rotated my favorite item in her fingers and used it to scribble notes on my chart.

Within minutes I was rushed to get a CT scan of my brain. It revealed nothing. The episode had calmed down by the time the results came back. Relieved, she sent me home. We had no answers. I returned to physical therapy, chiropractic, massages, and my Tylenol regimen.

Table of Physical Symptoms

I got up from the accident with several injuries. None of them were diagnosed during my brief stint in the emergency room on the day of the accident. It took several weeks for the first ones—sprain/strain to my spine—to be identified and an entire year before the wacko symptoms of the brain injury were professionally considered and addressed. A far cry from the three weeks I consciously gave my body to return to normal.

Symptom/Location	Duration
A burning sensation from the middle finger to the pinky on my left hand, all the way up my left arm and past my left shoulder.	5 years
A dark bruise on my right ankle, two inches thick, wrapped around the entire ankle.	3 years
Headaches, head pain, ice pick headaches and other vertical intense head pain.	5 years
Continuous full-body aches and pains.	5 years
Pain in my left shoulder, all around and in the joint.	5 years
Pain between my left scapula and spine that felt like something was torn or broken.	5 years

Damage to C6 and C7 and the disk between. Slight movement of vertebrae to the left.	Permanent
Two compromised vertebrae, one in my lower mid-back and one in my mid-back, impeding bending and twisting movements.	Permanent

Chapter Three

The Hidden Symptoms

There were symptoms hiding among the cacophony of physical ailments that grabbed my attention. I could not find the right words to describe them in a way my doctors could understand. I needed someone who could read between the lines. Someone who could hear the meaning behind the words I was using.

I was a physical person tuned into my physical body and what I could see with my eyes. It never occurred to me that my nervous system and brain function could be affected. I hadn't realized how much I took my thought processes for granted until I didn't have them anymore. Until that moment my thoughts defined me and I couldn't imagine my life—indeed, my Self—without that way of being. I wish I had the words to paint the picture with enough accuracy to describe the reality of losing oneself. I experienced the loss as the bottomless depths of an abyss, a chaotic void, an experience so deep and profound that it's rare to find your way back out.

I started staring off into space. I was alarmed when I first noticed this new habit. I was suddenly aware my attention was locked visually on a speck on the wall. I was at home in my living room and didn't know how long I had been fixated on it. I was only aware of being captivated by the speck. It began with my awareness of it becoming prominent, then I had the sensation of going into it. I was gone. And suddenly I was back in my living room sitting on the couch.

At other times I watched my arm twitch. When trying to explain these new symptoms to a specialist, I reported my experience using the words *internal tremors*. I could feel the shaking deep in my core and it made me feel intense weakness. The doctor couldn't see it and decided it wasn't a *real* tremor.

I was also having a gripping sensation under my skull, on top of my brain in the left parietal region. This was the same area where my helmeted head hit the road during the final impact that brought the rest of my body to an abrupt halt. The sensation had movement like a wave and most resembled a contraction. It held me captive for its duration, during which I could do nothing until it released me and I could think and move my body again. I was informed there were no muscle cells on the brain, so it couldn't have been happening. It was dismissed.

Focus, Memory, Personality, Anger, Depression, Anxiety, and PTSD

This injury didn't just happen to me. Its impact profoundly affected my children, my extended family, and my co-workers.

Focus

I was having difficulty concentrating and was easily and constantly distracted. My focus was filled with physical pain. It was everywhere all the time.

Short-Term Memory

One of my biggest complaints since the accident can been reduced to three words: short-term memory. In those early days before I was properly diagnosed I couldn't remember how to do simple tasks like copying a file from one directory to another. This is common, simple stuff in the computing world.

I was participating in a training session with a database administrator. After the training he said, "There... You just copy the file to the new directory and that's it."

I repeated him, "Copy the file to a new directory."

"Yeah," he said, "It's that easy!" I could tell he was proud of himself for making a complex task so simple for us.

"Do I know how to copy a file from one directory to another?" I wondered aloud. The small group of six looked at me, puzzled. He had just shown us. Then I stood up and looked over the cubicle wall at Alannah, the other worker on my team. She was busy at her computer. "Hey, Alannah, did I know how to copy a file?"

She stopped and looked up at me. "I don't know, did you?" Then she went back to her task at hand.

Everyone had cleared out of my cubicle and I sat back down at my desk pondering the situation. Then finally deduced that I must have known how to copy a file because this company only hires the best of the best. This was a simple action, I had just been told, and I was working there, so I must have been hired. What?

I couldn't retain anything I was learning at work. It happened during another training session. This time it was a one-on-one with my direct manager. Everyone knew me as a quick learner. It was one of the things I enjoyed about myself and was a repeated accolade in my performance reviews. This time I had questions. My manager had repeated herself twice and ended with, "You got that?"

"Yeah, I got it, thank you!" And I repeated her motions on the keyboard.

"Good. Okay." She got up and walked away, and as she did so it felt as if she had taken my knowledge with her. By the time she walked to her office, two cubicles away, I suddenly didn't know how to do it anymore. Then I lost track of what I was doing altogether.

Alannah watched me quietly from the next cubicle and started again with her crazy behavior stories of the woman she knew with a brain injury. *Why does she keep on about this person?!* As if for the first time, I decided it was an annoying co-worker quirk and started searching my desk for my chapstick. My routine had my chapstick to the left of my computer monitor during the day and tucked into the drawer just below the keyboard after work hours. But for now my eyes couldn't find it and I couldn't remember where I kept it. Later I would learn my eyes no longer tracked correctly, so sometimes I would see the chapstick and sometimes I wouldn't.

Reading

At home I was having trouble reading big words and then little words during our nightly family ritual of reading at bedtime. My youngest, then six, spoke up, "You're tired, Mom, let me read to you awhile." I welcomed the new ritual of the kids taking turns reading to us at night.

At work I was having difficulty figuring out what the emails said. I couldn't see all the details the clients were providing, so I couldn't troubleshoot issues in a timely manner. I started to get called into the upper manager's office to discuss my job performance.

Awareness

My spatial ability was gone. I used to be able to visualize things in space and rotate them in my head. This came in handy in college biochemistry class when I could envision a molecule and rotate it in my mind's eye to answer complex test questions. Now I was having difficulty figuring out the placement of the furniture at home. At work I couldn't figure out how my office got so messy. Files found their way to the top of my desk but couldn't find their way back into the file cabinet. If something was out of sight or out of earshot I would forget about it.

I was at home when I recognized my new habit of only being aware of my immediate surroundings. It wasn't that I forgot I had children per se, it was that nothing existed beyond what was in my immediate vicinity. I always knew they were my children when I heard them and when I saw them as they bounded into the room.

Personality Shift

I lived in the *extreme present moment*. I laughed and then cried at the irony when I realized *this* was the lifestyle many people strive for. While some people spend great amounts of time in meditation to achieve this phenomenon, it only took me maybe a fraction of a second at impact.

My driven (Type A) personality was switched to a calm (Type B) personality. I realized I couldn't function in the Type A world anymore. This was painful as I loved my Type A world and would have stayed there, 'til death did us part. Persistence and pushing through barriers was no longer a trait that worked for me. Now it fumbled me up and took me down. Down to the depths of depression with suicidal ideation. Down to bouts of neurological overwhelm requiring days of quiet retreat in my darkened bedroom to recover. I required great amounts of time in quiet.

I was hypersensitive to any negative impact my behavior could have on my children and I went to great lengths to make sure they were okay. I started using audio and visual cues to remind me of important things. I always set the alarm to remind myself to pick the kids up from school. From the outside it looked like we were going along the same. Behind the scenes I was struggling.

Long-Term Memory

I wasn't remembering things that happened four years earlier. Conversations with neighbors and family contained unfamiliar descriptions of things I did and said. They described awkward situations and epic adventures that sounded like something I would do, yet I had no memory of it and thought they must have been kidding. I learned to hide my memory deficits in silent pauses with affirming nods, pointing gestures, and other distracting behaviors.

I was in a circle of friends and family in our front yard one evening. Laughter and talking filled the summer air. I started sharing a funny thing one of my kids had done. As the part of the story approached where my child's name came up I couldn't remember it, but I knew which kid, so instead of saying a name I pointed to my youngest child. The group burst out laughing, getting the punch line and not my memory failure. Except for my youngest, whose smile turned into a frown and whose eyes were filling with water. The wound was deep. My youngest looked directly at me and asked, "Mom, did you forget my name?" then turned away from the group and announced, "You don't love me anymore!" My heart broke. I was found out. While I didn't remember the name, my love was stronger than ever.

I loved my children from the moment I realized I was pregnant. We had always had a great connection. Before the accident and subsequent injuries our relationship had been punctuated with rough-and-tumble play. My youngest had a habit of climbing all over me like a jungle gym every time I sat down. Play-wrestling was one of our favorite activities. Upon greeting, we would run toward each other. It was great fun to be charged. My favorite was the catch at mid-jump. I would reach out for the catch and end it with a long, endearing hug. Often I would let the momentum of the capture swing us around and around. I would take delight in the hug and make snorting noises with a neck nuzzle. Ending with both of us laughing and squealing with great joy.

After the accident our rough-and-tumble play came to an abrupt halt. As the laughter would start and I recognized an incoming charge, I would be reduced to holding my arms out and saying, "No. No, Honey. Mommy's back is hurting. I can't pick you up." The day I forgot my youngest child's name was the last straw, and the conclusion regarding this change in my behavior reflected a loss in my love, as if that was ever possible. It took me over a year to figure out how to reconnect with my rough-and-tumble kid. It happened at a friend's party. We were watching a slideshow of a fellow cyclist's cross-country bicycle adventure. The tired youngin climbed up into my lap. We held each other close and I was soon rewarded by the familiar twitch that marked deep sleep. Once again we had found our place. *Precious.*

My oldest child was a jumper and a climber. He kept his jumping confined to the gigantic trampoline in our back yard. This was our favorite activity to do together. His masterful flips made it all look so easy. When the accident happened, the physical pain and injuries—as of then unidentified—had me sitting on the sidelines of the trampoline and watching. Every time I tried to join in my neck and back would reduce me to applauding from the sideline again.

When my oldest climbed, it was the big tree in the backyard and walls in the house. Our house was a 500 square foot one-bedroom shack circa 1943. The small hall was more of a stepping spot that connected the dining nook with doors to the bedroom and the bathroom. He liked to try out his shoes on the walls of that hall. A photo I took shows him climbing all the way up those walls, one foot on each and a hand on the ceiling, evidence of his out of the box thinking.

One particular adventure in climbing that pushed the limits just about stopped my heart. I heard his voice calling me outside, and while there was whimsy rather than alarm, I ran out to the back yard to find him. When I couldn't find him in the yard, panic set in. Suddenly I heard his delight-filled laughter and then an announcement, "Look up! Look up!" only to discover him a few feet from the top of the tree, three times the height of our house.

Quick to Rageful Anger

Along with the other changes I started noticing uncharacteristic rage-filled episodes that would come upon me suddenly. At first I wrote it off as stress from the divorce and dealing with my former spouse, but later came to understand its true source as a symptom of traumatic brain injury. I had handled the first year and a half after the divorce without sudden outbursts. After the accident, my usual slow-to-anger demeanor switched to quick, rageful bursts with horrendous words escaping my mouth before I could stop them. It was as if I opened my mouth and the words just flowed.

Communication and Interacting with My Environment

I felt disconnected. I was having difficulty communicating. I couldn't understand what people were saying to me; I heard the words, but they didn't connect. They floated around in the space where my brain used to be. When my brain could hold onto the words long enough, I would be enveloped in thought trying to decipher the meaning.

When I spoke I had trouble finding words. Well-meaning people would speak up to fill in the blank, which only interrupted my slow processing flow and derailed my thoughts. Frustrations abounded at not being able to get a full sentence out. Eventually I learned to play a kind of verbal charade when I couldn't find the word. I described everything about the word which would encourage the other person in the conversation to start guessing what I meant. They usually got a thrill figuring it out. These encounters ended with a celebratory "Yay!" from me and a smile on the face of the word winner.

I was unaware when I spoke inappropriately. This was bad for business, and when I was observed doing so I was called into my manager's office and informed that my verbiage was not professional and that they couldn't trust me. I was removed from answering incoming telephone calls. I was getting a lot of face time with upper management and a lot of wide-eyed looks from my co-workers. I didn't know what they were talking about, nor could I remember the instances in question.

My co-worker Alannah and the woman that watched me from a distance were actually the reason I went to a seminar about brain injury... *just to see*. I was sure it was going to be a waste of a Saturday, but the kids were with their dad and I had some time. However, when I heard the familiar stories of bizarre behavior and cognitive fatigue I found kindred spirits; people having the same difficulty I was experiencing. I was introduced to the maze they were working through to get to the better place. The woman running the workshop, Constance Miller, was a brain injury survivor herself and shared her story of how she was inducted into the brain injury club with lifetime membership.

This is where I met a knowledgeable attorney whom I hired, Fred Langer, whose experience as an emergency room nurse led him to study law and help people from another angle. During his days in the E.R., he witnessed brain trauma results firsthand. He shared,

"It's a strange thing. I've seen a kid come into the E.R. who lost a Dixie cup full of brain matter and get up and get on with life, and I've seen someone get a slight bonk to the head and never recover. Every brain injury is different." I would hear this last soundbite echoed by doctors and therapists over the years during my hopeful and exhausting recovery process: *"Every brain injury is different."*

Table of Hidden Symptoms

Below is a table of the hidden symptoms I was experiencing, which were affecting my reality but to which I was dissociated.

Symptom	Duration
Cognitive fatigue, which I experienced as mental and physical exhaustion.	Permanent, to variable degrees
Neurological overwhelm. Extreme sensitivity to lights and noise.	Permanent, to variable degrees
Short and long-term memory loss. 'Swiss cheese memory.'	Permanent
Spatial ability impairment	Permanent
Depression	Permanent, to variable degrees
Anxiety and worry; excessive anxious thoughts.	Permanent, to variable degrees

Internal weakness which feels like physical weakness, but is caused by the nervous system.	Permanent
Episodes of staring off into space.	About 4 years
The gripping contraction-like sensation on the top left side of my brain, at and around the site where my helmeted head connected with the pavement.	About 4 years
Issues with balance where I suddenly feel like I'm falling. I tilt to the side to catch myself and oftentimes run into walls and people.	Permanent

Chapter Four

Failure to Make Satisfactory Progress

In the months prior to my official diagnosis I had been in conversation with my manager about my job performance. He was questioning what happened to me, why I had not been performing at my stellar standard. Periodic performance reviews had started to reflect a different perspective of my abilities. The transition was being recorded in these reviews and reflected my slump since the accident.

May 20, 2002 was a Monday. My manager asked if I could stay a little late and meet with him and the department manager. I went into the meeting without a clue it would be my last.

By 5:00 p.m. everyone on the floor had cleared out, except Alannah, who was slowly gathering her things. When I was escorted out of the meeting no one was around to see my tears flowing in a slow, silent cascade down my cheeks. I followed my escort's directions to return the company bus pass, but asked how I was supposed to get home. My identification badge, with the cool swipe feature that unlocked important doors, had already been confiscated.

I was to gather my things under the silent and watchful eye of my manager. His eyes followed the floor but when he spoke his voice was firm. He was now void of the connection and busy conversation I had grown accustomed to as co-workers. I wasn't allowed to touch my computer. He rushed to put himself between me and the keyboard as I approached. His quick movement startled me. Then he announced I wasn't allowed to touch my desk or the drawers. Instead, I had to stay a safe distance away from everything.

I was directed to name the contents that belonged to me and point to which drawer it was in. He would then open the drawer just wide enough for my fingers to retrieve the items. The drawer below the keyboard held my chapstick and contact-wetting eye drops. The lowest drawer of the file cabinet held my snacks: an entire box of Friends cereal, a bag with one bagel left, a small container of almond butter and two bananas. I offered him one. He declined politely, his eyes still lowered. I was informed I needed to move quicker.

I wondered where my friend went. Before he was promoted to management we had been conversation buddies at the coffee and snack area. Where was his compassion? Did he really think I would try to bring the company down with a software time bomb? I loved this company. It was all beyond me. I walked quickly to the nearest exit with him closely in tow. I was released onto Third Street in Seattle like a fish being released back into the vast ocean. I turned and watched the big glass door close. It reminded me of a tomb door. I felt like I was being locked out, pushed into the afterlife. His hand was gripping the handle and he was pulling it to make it close faster. He didn't return my gaze. I watched him walk away. My coat in one hand and my arm looped in the strap of my backpack, I started fumbling for bus change.

"The reality is you will grieve forever. You will not 'get over' the loss of a loved one; you will learn to live with it. You will heal and you will rebuild yourself around the loss you have suffered. You will be whole again, but you will never be the same. Nor should you be the same, nor would you want to."

—Elizabeth Kubler-Ross and John Kessler

PART TWO

Habits

Definition: Habit

A habit is an established behavior. Thoughts are habitual. Events occur in our lives and we assign meaning to them. What we feel about something will dictate our thoughts and we will base our actions on those thoughts. Directing and focusing on one's feelings is the key to controlling our experience.

Chapter Five

The Diagnosis

Mild traumatic brain injury (MTBI) was the official diagnosis. I got the word and the explanation of all the findings from my neurologist on July 9, 2002, a year and a week after the accident.

It was the culmination of two weeks of detailed tests in various specialists' offices. An EEG, a SPECT scan, and the neuropsychological evaluation were the three tests that brought the most insight into what was happening for me. The findings revealed the deficits in scientific terms for what I had been experiencing as my new normal since the moment of impact. The EEG showed a slowing of electrical impulses in the left side of my brain in the temporal region. Axonal shearing was discovered at several sites where the regions of the brain connect; the result of the torquing, twisting, bumping, and sloshing of my brain as it bounced around inside my skull, hitting protuberances, twisting itself to points of tension and tearing the fibers that carry the electrical messages through the brain. The neuropsychologist's report revealed that my memory was still intact, but my brain was not able to pay attention long enough to take what was happening and store it in memory.

Mild, Moderate, Severe

At the time of my injury the medical experts described a brain injury by the length of time the patient was unconscious. 30 minutes or less results in a *mild* diagnosis. over 30 minutes results in a *moderate* diagnosis, while getting into calendar days graduates the unconscious recipient to *severe* status. The name is a misnomer. To the layperson it suggests the amount of damage caused, but this naming system does not reflect the degree to which it affects your life, nor does it describe the extent of the damage or the prognosis for recovery. When I heard the words of the diagnosis, "*mild* traumatic brain injury," my mind grasped for its meaning. There was a sigh of relief as I reacted to "*mild*," thinking it was the least of the three options. Then the flush of horror as it registered "*traumatic brain injury*." Brain damage.

I was in the neurologist's office a little over a year after the accident, answering his question of "How long were you unconscious?" I reflected back to the moment of impact and played it over. At the scene of the accident and then later in the emergency room, when paramedics and doctors asked me if I was unconscious, my brain registered this as a seriously ridiculous question. I was thinking in Hollywood terms of bandages wrapped around heads and people lying in hospital beds. That extent was not my experience. I believed I was awake the entire time, since *I was awake when the paramedics arrived! Geesh! So obvious!*

As I was putting the pieces of my puzzle together I had an 'a-ha' moment. Yes, the point where everything went black, where it registered in my experience as beyond peace and time, was me unconscious. Now to determine how long. This was one of my symptoms of brain damage: I was now a very literal person tied up in the actuality of everything and going to great lengths to answer questions and figure things out in minute detail. The cognitive therapist would come to identify it for me as *"getting lost in the minutia."*

Reliving the impact, I studied the detail with great intent and childlike honesty. Length of time? I don't know. How long did it take my body to be hit, go limp, embrace the hood of the lovely blue Honda Civic and land on the top of my helmeted head on the abrupt edges of the pavement? So much happened in the batting of an eyelash. I tried to count seconds—one thousand one, one thousand two—as I watched the accident play out over and over in my mind's eye. I was awake by the time paramedics arrived. My internal dialog was running: *How long does it take them to respond to an accident? I was a few blocks from the fire station.*

The neurologist watched me for a brief time and then helped out. "Less than thirty minutes?" he offered. The doctor's inquiry had pulled me out of the loop of trying to figure it out. The diagnosis of mild traumatic brain injury was official. I was referred to a psychologist to help me deal with the change in personality, a cognitive therapist to retrain my brain to focus long enough to form memories, and a vocational therapist to determine if and where I could work.

Chapter Six

Habit One: Listening

*I chose to listen to my inner wisdom: I reached inside myself, beyond
what was determined in the moment, to identify what I wanted to feel
and explore where that could take me.*

*Change your brain in any way...
and you will definitely change your lifestyle!*

It wasn't that I was in outright defiance of what I was being
told by the medical experts. It was an inner wisdom, masquerading
outwardly as denial, that refused to accept the life sentence I was
being told would be my certain future. The concept of traumatic
brain injury—TBI—was foreign to me. A cascade of questions
poured forth. This inquiry began my quest and ultimately would
become my journey to awakening.

What was this thing referred to as TBI? My naiveté of what brain
injury is and its effects was represented in my question, *Should I
invest in drool buckets?* This question is also reflective of my mindset
of the time, still very much aligned with the financial prowess I
had been practicing. Now I was wondering how this was going to
affect me and my family. Would it be with me my entire life, or
was there some sort of opt-out plan? After all, when the injury

occurred I was only 37 years old (six days away from my 38th birthday) a single mother raising two young children. *Nothing could be wrong with me!*

The horrifying reality of having a condition I didn't know anything about opened me to the possibility I was improperly diagnosed. Wouldn't it be easier to have a brain tumor? At least they could take it out, right? My thoughts reached for other maladies I perceived as curable. I wanted my life back, as it was before the injury. Anything to get out of the maze of symptoms I had been living with since the accident.

My brain was so caught up in the struggle of what was happening to me that I didn't have enough brain power left to work the therapies in a way that would help me progress. Antidepressants were prescribed to relax me enough to get through the recovery process. I wasn't much for medication, and while I didn't see the correlation between an antidepressant and healing my brain, I would eventually acquiesce in an attempt to do all I could to get my brains back.

My attorney's words echoed in my mind. *"Every brain injury is different."* I was holding out for the brain injury that let me return to my beloved life with computers in the corporate world so I could raise my children in financial comfort. It took me many years to find out this was not going to be my experience.

The thing about brain injury is that your life is in such flux that it is difficult to have a schedule and to keep it. By now I was in full swing, experiencing chronic fatigue, depression, PTSD, and cognitive exhaustion along with constant body and head pain. My body was not reading the cues correctly anymore. It wasn't regulating my temperature, I didn't know when I needed to use the bathroom, and the intense level of pain I was in was misinterpreted as hunger. As I ate, the temporary respite provided a positive experience. It brought my attention away from the suffocating, consuming pain and pushed it to background noise. However, within moments I would forget that I ate and the pain would return to the forefront of my existence. I would determine it must be hunger and I would eat again. This went on for about five years and resulted in a weight gain of 50 pounds.

At the age of 17 I had been exposed to Tony Robbins tapes. I had listened to them and laid out the list of things I wanted to have, do, and experience during my lifetime. I learned how to set and reach goals. I had developed organizational skills and a *can-do* mindset. I restructured my language to live into my dreams. One example of this was in how I used language and how that shaped my experience. I saw problems as insurmountable and situations as things to find a solution to. So I started inserting 'situation' into everything I had previously thought of as a 'problem.'

During this time I was motivated to write a letter of commitment to myself and my community where I declared I would provide a positive and lasting impact on society, albeit at the time I wrote the letter I was not sure how I was going to attain this goal. Nowhere on my list of dos, haves and bes was there "get hit by a car, sustain major lifestyle-changing injuries, and become a burden on society." In my mind, I was supposed to be the one that helped others, not the one getting help! And now I began to wonder: *how was I going to contribute positively to society if I had a brain injury?*

Chapter Seven
The New Normal

I was aware I was experiencing the world differently. It had to do with my senses. Sight, sound, smell, taste, and touch were all affected and this made a huge difference in my ability to interact with my environment and the people in it.

Differences in Seeing

I was noticing differences in how I saw the world visually. Things looked different. I couldn't explain it, and the regular examination of my eyes didn't reveal any physical damage. Later it would be discovered that my eyes were not tracking properly. Instead they focused in a random fashion that didn't allow my brain to register what it was seeing. This affected my ability to read and see objects in my environment.

My interest in photography increased as I was overwhelmed by seeing everything at once. I followed my internal urgings to take my camera out into nature. The photo adventure produced relief when I looked through the lens. I captured images in small increments then put them together to grasp the larger picture of the entire landscape.

Differences in Hearing: Post-Traumatic Dizziness and Hearing Loss

I was told it was common for the kind of impact I took to cause the inner ear bones to break. The physical examination of my ears showed both tympanic membranes intact, but the bones were on the mend. I sustained permanent conductive hearing loss in my left ear and my inner gyroscope had been knocked off center and needed to be rebalanced. This was done through vestibular rehabilitation. While the rehab helped with the majority of my balance issues, I still experience the occasional loss of stability that results in stumbling and bumping into walls.

Differences in Taste and Smell

Food tasted different. Some things I didn't like before the injury I found myself gravitating toward and enjoying. My senses of taste and smell were heightened and I was experiencing a whole new set of sensory delights and intrusions.

Differences in Personality: Type A to Type B

My old tactic of pushing through tough situations that had served me well at my corporate job didn't work anymore. I could no longer handle the pressure of deadlines. Too much emotional stimulation would lead to neurological overwhelm; my brain would simply shut down and stop thinking. My habit of working with a forceful, continuous drive eventually gave way to a relaxed, calm progression of thought that allowed the way to show itself.

Ginger Hurt was the vocational therapist who did the testing to see what kind of work I could do, if any. I was at a point where I had people telling me what I couldn't do and I just wanted someone to point me in a direction. After our testing I asked Ginger, "What *can* I do?" She said she gets that a lot, but it was something I would need to figure out on my own. It wasn't as simple as just being told what to do. She wrote a report for the insurance company but told me not to read it for three months. I waited. When I read it I wept. Prognosis was not good. Based on the tests I wasn't expected to return to regular employment and it suggested I seek out volunteer work to be of service to help me feel better. I resisted. I wanted to earn money, not work for free!

An Excerpt from the Functional Assessment Report

Goal areas for treatment have included the following:

Design and implementation of strategies for more effective home management. This included: shopping, meal planning, and cooking; money management; parenting skills; design and implementation of a comprehensive organizational and memory system to manage daily life, tasks, paperwork, etc.

Adjustment to disability counseling with a focus on identifying viable employment options that are consistent with Ms. Marcum-McCoy's current cognitive abilities.
Provision of resource referral as appropriate.

Generalization of gains made in clinical cognitive rehabilitation services to real-life settings such as home and school.

Goal-setting and treatment was guided by information provided by Ms. Marcum-McCoy's cognitive rehabilitation therapist, Patricia Youngman, MS, and review of the neuropsychological evaluation results of Dr. Goodwin's testing completed in July, 2002. Dr. Goodwin delineated the following cognitive difficulties: (1) impaired attention/concentration; (2) deficits in concept formation and cognitive flexibility; (3) difficulties with auditory concentration and discrimination of word-sounds in conversation; and (4) problems with sequencing and speed of information processing. Some difficulties were also noted with working memory most likely secondary to attention problems.

FUNCTIONAL COGNITIVE REHABILITATION SERVICES:

Mia Marcum-McCoy was seen for diagnostic interview on August 23, 2002. At that time, she was participating in formal cognitive rehabilitation services with Patricia Youngman, MS, CCC-Sp, Cognitive Therapist, working on the goals of attention and concentration; speed of information processing; memory; and auditory processing. Goals for functional cognitive rehabilitation are outlined above. Specific interventions were:

- Development of daily, weekly and monthly methods for managing her household.
- Development of a memory system to include a Day Timer planner.
- Development of a queuing system to insure task completion.

- Re-organization of her home environment for ease of access.
- Development of systems for bill paying, banking and other record keeping.
- Development of systems for shopping, meal planning and cooking.

Ms. Marcum-McCoy was motivated and fully participated in functional cognitive rehabilitation services. However, she continues to demonstrate cognitive difficulties which impact her ability to manage her home and work life effectively. These include:

- Cognitive fatigue which impacts her ability to fully utilize cognitive skills.
- Emotional lability.
- Difficulties concentrating secondary to chronic fatigue and pain.
- Visual difficulties, e.g., trouble with visual tracking and attention to small detail.
- Deficits in short-term memory.
- Impaired ability to multi-task.
- Difficulty completing tasks that involve sequencing in unstructured environments.
- Problems with organizing, planning and setting priorities.
- Slowed speed of processing information.

During functional cognitive rehabilitation services, Ms. Marcum-McCoy demonstrated the ability to use a written compensation system for memory difficulties. She, however, remains challenged by tasks or projects requiring high level organizational skills. Multi-tasking is very difficult, especially in the presence of distractions. She requires assistance when making decisions that require consideration of multiple variables.

ASSESSMENT RESULTS:

Results of this assessment indicate that Ms. Marcum-McCoy continues to demonstrate cognitive, physical and psychosocial difficulties which significantly impact her ability to function as a single parent, manage her household and return to employment. Although she made gains in cognitive rehabilitation, she continues to have cognitive deficits which impact her success, both vocationally and in her activities of daily living.

* * *

The professional reports had their own language to describe the details of the challenges I was and would be facing. Below is an excerpt from my journal, describing 'a day in the life.' At this time I had already been terminated from my beloved employment and I was trying to retrain into another position while also participating in several therapies.

An Excerpt from My Journal

February 4, 2003 (1 ½ years after the accident)

My home has been extremely cluttered (more than usual) and the clutter is overwhelming yet I don't seem to be able to get it clean. I have some systems set up and I can get the dishes done and do laundry two to three times a week.

An example of a difficult day for me: I was fixing myself something to eat. I washed an apple and put it in the dish drainer to dry. When I turned my back on it, I forgot about it. I decided I needed toast and put the bread in the toaster. I turned my back to do something else and forgot about the toast. I started fixing a bowl of cereal with milk and eating it. Then, I heard the toast pop up and looked in the direction of the noise... seeing the toast, I remembered I was making it.

I put the bowl of cereal down, walked to the toaster, took it out and buttered it and cut it in half. I started eating one-half piece of the toast and turned my back to the plate. Walked to the table four steps away stood there while I finished the piece of toast in my hand. Turned, walked toward the sink, saw the apple and remembered that I washed it to eat. So I took a bite.

My youngest child called to me. I walked two steps to the table and set the apple down, answered the question and forgot about the apple in front of me. I walked through the kitchen and spotted my cereal bowl on the stove top. Picked it up and started eating it. Later the apple fell off the table and my youngest child said, "Whoops, the apple fell." I turned, looked at the apple and remembered that I had been eating it. Better to have returned to bed, but I have two children that need me this day. So, the day just went on and on like this.

I have three loads of clean laundry piled in my bedroom. I remember it only when I see it. I will need to put it in my schedule to get it folded and put away. Patty Youngman taught me to schedule things to remind me to do them. I have put the schedule in a place that I will see it so I can remember to look at it.

When I was 17 years old, I taught myself how to make lists, organize and complete tasks to reach my goals. So it is strange to me that I am where I am now... without a clue that I need to relearn how to do this. I don't know how to do it and I am not aware that I don't know, nor where to start. Someone else has to initiate and suggest it in the first place. Example: when I was working, my supervisor asked me if I had seen my doctor for my head/brain when I told him that since the accident I felt like someone took a full garbage can and emptied it on me and I can't get out. After he said that, I got the clue to call my doctor and make an appointment.

Recently, I had trouble figuring out how to get my kids to the eye doctor. It has been two months since my youngest started experiencing blurry vision. I asked the kids' father to find out what the health coverage was (since I lost my job the children are on their father's health insurance). He just told me, "It's simple, call the number on the back of their insurance cards and find out if they are covered for vision and where to go". It took me another two weeks to figure out how to do it from his instructions.

At School

Even though I earned a Master's degree with a significant GPA and having researched, written, defended and published my thesis, The Challenge to Breastfeed in the United States (1998 Western Washington University), I have had to relearn how to take notes. (Ginger Hurt taught me the Cornell method). I keep a sample copy of 'how-to' with me and when I forget the process, I look at the copy. I have forgotten that I have a copy at times only to find it when I dig through my files or am reminded by Ginger. I have as yet to use it as I have been taught. I start out with good intentions but somehow in the process of me taking notes during lecture everything becomes jumbled and I feel lucky to get anything on paper at all. Sometimes during note taking in lectures, I will hear something that I want to note and by the time my pencil gets to paper I have forgotten what it was I was going to write.

I have a small plastic carrying file cabinet that I keep hanging files for each class. I have included a file for each text so I can see if I have a book for that class or not. I take it with me to school so I have everything with me at all times. I am afraid of forgetting something I need for class or to study. Each hanging file has files for class syllabus, handouts, lecture notes, assignments. I write assignments and due dates in my [day planner] schedule which I carry with me everywhere. Ginger, my vocational therapist, helped me set up and work this system.

I keep everything in my schedule and look at it often throughout the day to remind me what I am to do and when. I color coat times scheduled for study, naps, when my children are with their father. I have been taught (by Patty Youngman) how to use this tool. I have needed help in figuring out how to organize my days and how to schedule to get things done.

I was born in Kirkland, Washington, have lived in the area for most of my life and so, am very familiar with this town and surrounding areas. I have been to Lake Washington Technical College campus many times. On my second week of classes, I was on my way to college and suddenly, I forgot how to get there. From my cell phone in my car, I called a friend who helped me figure out a way to get to school. Although I left in plenty of time to settle in before class started, I was 30 minutes late to class because I suddenly forgot how to get there.

I often have the feeling of being "disconnected." Some days are worse than others. The best days are when I don't have much on my calendar for the week; I take my daily 1.5 hour naps, and look at my calendar often. Patty Youngman and Ginger Hurt have been instrumental in getting me this far.

Chapter Eight
Strategies Emerging

After several years and a lot of rehabilitation my brain's ability to focus had increased some but not much. This was evident in my family's everyday world as we used the practice of drive-through dining to test my memory. We tracked my progress by drive-through orders. We celebrated with loud cheers when I could remember and "next time" when I didn't. The test would start with my excited voice as we approached the drive-through. "Let's test Mom's memory!" It was like I was announcing a game show. Everyone was eager to participate.

The game was like *telephone,* a game I played in my youth, where one person would start with a sentence and each person would tell what they heard to the next person in line. In that game, what the last person heard was usually not what the first person said. The difference I was having in my version was that I couldn't remember what was said to me to relay it to the next person.

In those early attempts, the one word being relayed would slip out of my mind during the process of turning my head and my attention from the child to the reader board microphone. After two failed attempts I would lean back in my seat and motion for the child to yell out their own order. With practice I was able to remember one item at a time and would delight in being able to relay a disjointed but complete order. After many months of therapy and lots of practice at playing the drive through game, my success at reciting one child's entire order was met with an eruption of cheers. *Progress.*

About the time the doctor started referring to my lifestyle of symptoms as post-concussive syndrome, my eldest child asked, "Mom, when is the brain not injured anymore? Even if it doesn't heal to how it was before, when is the injured way of being considered normal?" Excellent question! I raised intelligent children. My new normal was defined by the neurological overwhelm I experienced when the lights were too bright, the noise level was too loud, or there were too many people. I would erupt into tears of frustration if I could not get myself to a quiet, darkened space to calm down.

My oldest child was instrumental in assisting me on those noisy, confined car trips when I was suddenly on the verge of a meltdown. I was overcome with rage, another symptom of brain injury. That was the day I realized I was verbally out of control. Damaging words suddenly spewed from my mouth. I didn't know what I was saying. I was hearing the words at the same time my children were being exposed to them. By the look on their faces I could see they were as horrified as I was. The palm of my right hand pressed against my mouth in an attempt to stop the damage.

To this point my children had been raised sheltered from verbal abuse. From this incident was born my new meltdown strategy. That first day I apologized and told the children, "Mommy needs a timeout and we all need to be quiet," which was met by the youngest child's question: "But for how long?" My overstimulated brain could not make sense of the words. They swirled and floated in my mind but would not connect. The eldest child must have seen the look on my face as he turned around to get the younger child's attention in the back seat behind me and stated firmly, "Be quiet!"

There was silence for a few minutes until I could feel myself calm down enough to function again and I said, "Okay, you can talk now," in a happier, more relaxed tone. From then on, when I would feel the overwhelm creep up I would be able to tell the children I needed a timeout, which meant everyone got to be silent until I said otherwise. They would wait, mostly patiently, for the noise curfew to lift. This is how we have dealt with looming neurological meltdowns since.

Neurological overwhelm played itself out in an assortment of ways. I mostly recognized it with overstimulation of visual and auditory functions. Below are some of the strategies that emerged.

Making Decisions

I would call my mother or sister when I was having difficulty making a decision and they would talk me through it. An example of this was when I was shopping for laundry soap. I became overwhelmed by the amount of choices and colors that filled the store aisle. I started to cry. I hid my frustration from fellow shoppers near me while I pulled out my cell phone and called my sister. She asked questions so I could come to a decision. Finally, she directed me to find the name of the soap she knew I used.

Overstimulation While Shopping

When I went shopping for groceries, I shopped from a list to remember what I needed. Even so, I became confused when more than five ingredients lined my shopping cart. My brain could only handle a few items at a time. I made frequent trips to the store. I would also become overwhelmed by the bright lights and loud noises and would need to get myself out of the store as soon as possible. My strategy for this was to get myself to the car and pull a blanket or my coat over my head, which would immediately relieve visual overwhelm. I'd hold my ears closed in the dark until I could come back to calm. *Relief.*

Preparing Meals

My ability to cook diminished. I had difficulty figuring out what to do especially if I was missing an ingredient. It threw me into frustration. When this happened, I directed the kids to get into the car for drive-through dinning. We did this four to six times per week.

While my vocational counselor was doing a home visit, she observed me attempting to cook. Watching my difficulty, she figured out my eyes didn't track the page of the cookbook and this was creating great challenge in preparing a recipe at all.

My short-term memory was almost nonexistent. I could start a pot of water boiling on the stove, turn away from it, and forget it. More than once the smell of smoke brought me back to the kitchen, only to see the pot engulfed in flame.

Sleeping Habits

My new normal took up my days and nights. I oriented myself by where I woke up, sleeping in my bed at night and napping on the couch during the day, so when I woke up I would know if I had been sleeping from the evening or from the daytime.

I usually slept 14 to 20 hours a day and supplemented with one or more naps lasting anywhere from 20 minutes to four hours. Well-meaning people hearing my need for a nap would ask, "Don't you sleep well at night?" I heard a lot of advice on how to make myself stay awake during the day so I could experience more rest-filled nights. However, my naps during the day were predicated by bouts of cognitive exhaustion. How could anyone know what this was like unless they experienced it themselves? I would not wish this experience on anyone. When people commented on how they *couldn't imagine*, I would simply say, "I am so glad you can't."

Chapter Nine

Habit Two: Acceptance

"It feels like the information is in there," pointing to my brain, "but the bridge to get to it is out."

The trauma to my brain had caused the nerve highways called axons to shear. The information was still in there, but the road the message traveled was out. It was going to take some time to rebuild an alternative pathway if it was going to happen at all. My life had not returned to my previous normal, so it became my task to incorporate what normal is for me now and what it would be in each moment. I could not accept my life as it was; however, I could accept a shift in perspective.

I wanted my old life back. I thought if I dutifully followed the advice and guidance of the experts in white coats, my chances of recovery would be greater. These authorities see brain injury every day. I thought, they should be able to tell me if I would get back my precious functioning and how much, right? As it turns out, this is not the case. No one can tell anyone how their life is or will be. It is up to each of us to define that for ourselves and be courageous enough to step into that life.

By now both professionals and family members were stressing my need to *"just accept it."* I was assured life would go much easier if I stopped fighting it. Nobody, including me, understood that I could not accept any of it with the level of understanding I had at that time. I thought they were asking me to acquiesce, to give up, give in, and live the life I was being told by others was my certain future. There was no solace in that life. I had to find my own way. I had to shift perspectives to come to acceptance.

I had to rewrite my life. I was still running on a corporate America mentality that no longer served me. In fact, it was the cause of increased frustration and mental anguish each time I relived how I didn't measure up, how I wasn't the same person I longed to be and worked toward being. I fell absolutely short. In corporate terms I was a failure, although my mental programming didn't accept failure and I was turning inward on myself. My thoughts of suicide increased in frequency. I was going to the dark side. Two events steered me from this fate: first, I had guidance from a knowledgeable counselor who shared with me the reality of children who are survived by a parent who commits suicide. The children suffer in agony their entire lives. The thought of causing my children pain was a stringent deterrent. Second, a divine intervention came when a telephone call from my brother stopped my initial process. It gave me another chance at living fully in this life.

Acceptance started as I began engaging in life. I stepped into the flow. At first I fought the current, then after time I learned to let go and be amazed at what showed up.

Definitions

It all started with definitions. I had learned this lesson—pre-injury —by 1998 while in graduate school writing my master's thesis. Most people use the same words but mean different things. In my thesis I started with definitions to make sure everyone knew what I meant by the terms I used. I did this so the reader understood my research. It provided common ground and a reference point.

There was no forewarning of the differences in definitions between the three entities that work so closely together in my brain injury world. I was shocked to learn the intricate nuances between legal, medical, and insurance verbiage. The only definition that was missing from the equation was my own, and this golden nugget would change my life beyond what was previously visible.

Totally disabled. The reality of the words were hard to comprehend as I read them on the page. It looked like a label or a brand rather than reality of status. This was the legal system's determination after two grueling years with no improvement. The medical community allowed a little more time and a lot more rehabilitation hours. The insurance company had their own version of what disability is, and their own set of criteria to decide if and when *they* would determine my ability to work. I learned this determination is independent of the reality of a person actually being hired to perform the tasks. Their constant contact with endless questions and paperwork felt more like harassment, with reminders of how I didn't measure up rather than a sincere attempt to rebuild me and return me to the workforce and a job I could actually do successfully and sustainably. I could feel the confusion set in and observed how listening to any of them could drive a person nuts! Instead, I chose to listen to my inner wisdom: I reached inside myself to identify what I wanted to feel and explore where that could take me.

After four-plus years of deliberate and industrious rehabilitation my doctor informed me that they had done everything they could for me to get my brain function back. It was determined my brain was too injured to return to work. I had been officially graduated and was released from the rehabilitation team's care. I was told, "Go home, enjoy your children, and the life you have." I love my children and yet this was only part of the equation for me to live a full life. My life was supposed to include children *and* the gratifying, meaningful work that I associated with gainful employment.

I had worked since I was 11 years old. It was ingrained in me. I equated work with earning a healthy income and I had just begun to earn substantial amounts when my life was irreversibly interrupted. I would have allowed a brief inconvenience, but I was not prepared for a life sentence. Who would be? I needed to reevaluate my strengths and weaknesses and address getting on with living.

I wouldn't find that piece of the puzzle until 2013, when a serendipitous move across the state would bring me closer to people living with brain injury and a process to redefine myself. For now I was on my own paying $118 per hour to a psychologist I really liked, but with whom I was reliving the accident and frustration at not being who I was before. I was told I was a classic case. The unusual thing about me that drew the most concern from the psychologist was my stress level. It measured three times the level of the most stressful job; professional firefighters.

All Life Has Value

Looking back over my life I can see the pattern of returning to nature for connection, especially during times of stress. During this phase I was drawn out into the garden for lessons and healing. One day I was in the garden, therapeutically pulling weeds, thinking about life and the conversation I'd had with the doctor about the health risks I faced based on the traumatic brain injury diagnosis. I was told 99.9% of people who sustain TBI have depression: "*It's just part of the package.*" He also informed me I had a greater than normal risk of diabetes, hypertension, early onset dementia, and Parkinson's disease. There were others, but these were the ones I remembered.

The sun was shining upon me and the weed roots were letting go of the soil with each gentle tug. I was in an emotional upheaval, stricken with disbelief at the thought that this was how my life would end up. I believed I had been born to do great things. Again, I found myself wondering, *How am I going to contribute positively to society with this brain injury?* My mind was on children, fairness, and how long and short people's lives can be. The question sprouted, *What about children that are born with the inability to walk and talk, being bound to a wheelchair, unable to ever care for themselves?* The conversation I was having with the Divine returned with thoughts that flowed like pristine water: *All life has value. Those individuals may be teaching the ones around them; perhaps compassion, service, unconditional love. Reflecting the gift of love is a caregiver's primary role.* We each have a role to play.

If I'm Not Working, Then What Am I?

I had been kept alive by the fantasy of finding the job that would accommodate all the limitations set upon me by the physical and cognitive aspects of brain injury. When I started to engage in the life in front of me I learned many things. I was open to seeing what was not previously available to me. The lesson I learned was that I placed value in myself based on what I could achieve, which meant what I could *do*. In my previous life, before brain injury, I was quite accomplished at doing. I mastered so many skillsets necessary for the busy, mentally active person on the go with two kids, a full-time job, a household to run, and a pregnant cat.

I found it embarrassing to tell the same *why-I-am-not-working* story when asked, "So... What do you do?" My answer would have to be, "I look for things," or "I sleep a lot and get neurologically overwhelmed and cry, how about you?" So I put a spin on it. I deduced that if I was not working then I was retired, and because I was in computers at my last job, acquaintances put together stories they heard about early Microsoft millionaires and retirement at a young age. Hey, I much preferred the fantasy version too... but my bank account did not reflect millionaire status and Microsoft was not the company I had worked for. Still, it was easier to say a few pleasant words than to dredge up the whole scenario of how I came to not work and my eternal sadness and frustration over the whole mess.

What Do Retired People Do?

I was not pleased with what I heard from the medical community, but they did their best and they had exhausted their expertise. There was nothing left for them to do. I needed mentors, examples of how I could live a productive life, and support to live that life. I needed hope.

I began to think about my options. What do retired people do? The answer came quickly and surprised me. *Anything they want!* Okay, what *do* I want to do? *Ski, travel, play guitar, tap dance.* Skiing was out. The injuries to my neck, back and left shoulder were a source of constant pain. I was angry. I had been a very physically-oriented person, but now I couldn't move, sit, stand or stoop without some perpetual reminder of my losses.

Travel

Short excursions helped me embrace life with brain injury from a new perspective. My children and I started talking about places we wanted to go and things we wanted to experience. This encouraged the feeling of freedom and an opening began to emerge: living a brain injury lifestyle was not necessarily being sentenced to a life of misery. Enjoyment was coming back into our lives. My youngest child wanted hotel beds we could jump on and we all wanted a swimming pool. I was partial to scenery that included big water. Our short excursions took us to the Olympic Peninsula in Washington State, Harrison Hot Springs Resort in Canada, and the Yucatan Peninsula in Mexico. We were planning a trip to Japan, but I let the fear of an extended stay in unfamiliar and crowded spaces stop us.

Play Guitar

I had first been exposed to playing guitar around the age of eight when my mother showed me and my siblings a few chords. In seventh grade it was an elective class I enjoyed. Now my eldest child, Tony, was thirteen years old and wanted to learn. I chose it as a bonding experience and signed us both up for electric guitar lessons through the community center. My youngest took private drum instruction from a band member who came to our home and practiced on the full set I'd purchased specifically for my youngest but we all enjoyed.

My kids and I laughed and played and made up songs with and without the aid of electric guitars and the drum set. My stage name became Can-D Rappa. Most of my songs were about kids cleaning their rooms and always ended with my arms folded in a sideways rapper stance, "Clean your room! Mom'A'2 Kids." Or some public service announcement, "Look both ways before you cross the street. Mom'A'2 Kids."

During guitar class, Tony excelled while I struggled with memory. I kept the cheat sheet in front of me at all times. It didn't matter how much I practiced; I was slow. I was literally relearning each time I played. I was proud of Tony, he was thriving. He continued with private lessons and a higher quality guitar. His career as a musician was born. His lessons inspired his dad to follow his own childhood desire to learn guitar—a desire I encouraged during our marriage but a calling he hadn't answered until now, with the encouragement and some pointers from his son.

Tony's love of music started with the violin in fifth grade and advanced with electric and acoustic guitar, then on to keyboard, drums, and bass. With the aid of his Apple computer and GarageBand software, he wrote and produced his first CD at the age of 14, and a few years later, his second CD and further education as a sound engineer. He is a successful musician, sound engineer, and graphic artist. His skills have helped several musicians get their music out into the world. He has also designed product art for several books, DVDs, and CDs. Tracing it all back, I can see how you never know who your actions are going to help.

Tap Dancing to a New Definition of Success

When I decided to learn to tap dance I gravitated toward the senior center. I didn't know where else to go. I couldn't find any classes for young retired people. At 40ish, I was the only one with dark hair in a sea of grey, silver, and white. I felt sorry for the woman at the head of the class, obviously a talented dancer and gifted instructor. She was in her prime at 78 years young. She was conscientious and determined we would *all* learn the steps. I was enjoying the tap, tap, tapping, but soon realized I was not going to remember those moves. Instead of focusing on the frustration of that, I joyously moved my body around while making impressive tap noises and thinking about the Hollywood movies that featured tap dancing I watched in my youth.

I didn't learn the tap routines—I couldn't recall them—but I did learn to redefine success. In my enjoyment of the corporate world, my personal mantra and the definition of success was *'exceeding excellence'* with my *can-do* attitude and solution-based mentality. It was proper for that environment and these served me; they made me stronger and propelled me to greater heights, but now those words no longer translated to anything meaningful out here where I recognized limitations and losses at every turn.

To this point, my daily living experience brought torment and frustration. My change in definition allowed me to gain some much needed relief. Now the simple act of enjoying whatever I was participating in at the moment was Success. This marked the transition from my *doing* to my *being* state of mind. Sensating in JOY was all I needed to be successful!

If I Could Just Find the Right Job

I kept thinking if I could just find the right job I could return to lucrative employment—or the right hobby where I could feel like my old self—but I took the brain and bodily injuries everywhere I went and into every endeavor. The most persistent and invasive was my short-term memory issue. My long term memory was also affected. It became a running joke and I looked for various ways to impart the same information of "I don't remember." It wasn't that I didn't want to, it was that the bridge was out and I didn't have access to that information anymore. My brains processing speed was also affected. Sometimes acquaintances or friends would make a comment, "If you don't want to answer the question just say so!" And when I would take too long to answer, "Come on, it's not rocket science, Mia!" or "If it takes you that long to think of something to say, I can't wait to hear this lie!" It was embarrassing. The isolation of the impairment reestablished itself with each snide retort.

I was trying to return to the workforce and volunteered to see if I could do the tasks of an event coordinator. It seemed simple enough. The woman in charge asked me to do something and I attempted to carry it out. It was not to her specifications, so I asked her to repeat the directions she had given me previously. I informed her I had a head injury and it just takes a little longer for my brain to process the information.

She began to speak to me again. This time SO M-U-C-H L-O-U-D-E-R AND S—L—O—W—E—R. I watched her mouth in fascination. It started with her lower lip dressed in red lipstick. Then I noticed the corners of her mouth and the upper lip. Her mouth moved in slow motion. I was captivated by her booming voice until suddenly—I laughed out loud. I realized she had no idea what I was talking about and I was unable to convey what was happening for me.

This was the norm in my life now. I was usually left feeling frustrated and isolated by these experiences, and yet when trying to convey this frustration I would be met with, "If you keep thinking you have a brain injury, you're just going to reinforce it and keep it longer." Huh? I was just trying to express what was going on for me. So, I was not supposed to speak about it and I was not supposed to think about it, yet it was the focus of my moment-to-moment existence. I needed a new focal point.

Chapter Ten
Habit Three: Focus

What we focus on expands.

I feel JOY when…
I see colorful flowers in the garden,
I smell the fragrant plants,
I feel the texture of leaves,
I hear the sounds of birds,
I taste the morning dew off the crisp green leaves.

It was a tumultuous time. My body was still racked with a level of pain equal only to my desire and determination to live a higher quality of life; one filled with joy. Until this time I had been trying to figure out what I *could* do with the definitions of *lack* and *limitation* bestowed upon me by the legal, medical, and insurance companies. These were terms they used simply so they could do their business, but I had adopted them as my own and was attempting to use them to put the pieces of my life back together. As it turns out, I was not able to build a life around these terms and I had to find my own way and restructure my own language to build a life I could truly call my own.

Those early years of using lack-filled and limiting vocabulary led me to wonder what I *could* do and what I would ever be capable of again. Memories of how I *used to be* compared to how I was now did not serve me. I had changed in that instant of impact and now I was coming to understand what it truly meant for me and my family. It didn't have to be a game stopper. I had to let go of the belief that my life was better before. I could not exist in the 'less than I was before' life. No one could be expected to contribute if their minds are always focused on the negative. I had to let go of the idea that the superpowers of multitasking and problem solving I had before were the best parts of me, even though they *were* in every job I held for over twenty years. Now I couldn't imagine my life without writing everything down to remember it. I felt the grip of loss lessening.

I still didn't understand the totality of what was happening to me and I had been living this brain injury experience for several years. If living it was what it took to have a grasp at understanding its devastation, I was grateful that others could not relate, though I was isolated by my inability to express myself. I was having great difficulty connecting with people. My isolation redirected my outward experience to an inward journey and I began to commune with nature and to experience the solace and deep, satisfying peace that followed my adventures in the garden, in the woods, and in the lake water.

There came a time when my brain and body finally settled down enough for me to be able to read again. It was after much cognitive therapy and retraining my eyes to scan the page properly so my brain could translate. I could usually understand as I was reading, but because it didn't get stored in short-term memory, I had the joy of new ideas and learning all over again. My neurotic-like pacing—*walking the house*—relaxed a bit and allowed me to watch longer and longer segments of movies. Several topics piqued my interest and provided puzzle pieces for me to put my life and dreams back together. As I followed my interests, a shift appeared, and one door of opportunity after another began to open as I simply walked down the hallway.

Opening to Possibility: *Post Concussion*

I was walking through the video store looking for a movie when my eyes fixed on the word *Concussion*. I had that! I am forever grateful for Daniel Yoon and his award-winning movie, *Post Concussion*. A write-up from an anonymous critic called it "a semi-autobiographical film, brutally funny, unsentimental yet oddly inspiring portrayal of one man's journey after a serious head injury."

It was the first time since the injury I realized people with brain injury can have a big, positive impact and I began to believe it was possible for me. I watched my life unfold on the screen through this character. I felt an immediate connection with and appreciation for Daniel. I was even more impressed to learn from the outtake interviews of the persistence and the creativity that Daniel went through to make the movie. His personal sharing of what it took, how he did it, and the mistakes that turned out to make the movie what it was allowed me to open to another path of possibilities. Daniel was an example for me of how a person with brain injury can start from where they are, utilize resources around them, and leverage their habits to reach a goal and live a new dream.

Making a Conscious Decision: *Choosing Joy in the Midst of Chaos*

The book *Choosing Joy in the Midst of Chaos* by Dolly Mae was my inspiration to *choose joy* in every moment. From the official synopsis: "Change will always happen. It's how we meet that experience that determines who we really are. This book shows how to find joy and remain happy when life seems to bring more than we can endure. No matter what we experience: heartache, illness, despair, grief, loss or financial struggle, *Choosing Joy* shows us how to regain our balance and be happy once again."

I was drawn to this book about the same time I had been told the devastating news there was nothing more the rehabilitation team could do. This book helped me to see joy as a choice and that I could choose it in any situation at any time. It was a deliberate process—a conscious decision. I was outside in the grass, looking down and thinking about what the doctors told me and I was feeling especially angry. The juices of the anger were mixing with my gut telling me *this isn't the life I'm meant to lead.* My internal dialog raged: *THIS is MY life! This is the only one I know of. This one*

*happening right now. I WANT A LIFE FILLED WITH JOY! So,
even though I have this thing called brain injury and my life has gone
in a direction I don't recognize, I am CHOOSING to live a joy-filled
life. This is my life, so this is MY JOY-FILLED LIFE.*

Believe in a Possibility

By this time, I was also being exposed to the movie, *The Secret*, and
then not too far behind that, *What the #$*! Do We Know!?*, the
former providing a set of skills to practice and the latter providing
scientific reason to believe in the possibility. I *love* science! I began
to believe at the cellular level and the new shift was palpable. As a
young athlete I was already familiar with the power of the mind
and mental imaging for the purpose of increasing athletic abilities.
I had also been exposed to imagining people, places and things I
wanted to experience and had used that when I was 17 years old to
guide my life. By the time I was 20 I had experienced all those
people, places and things... except the Corvette. I had just never
used the technique to this extent before. Now I was using it to
shift my entire experience from misery to fulfillment.

When I started with my desire for a joy-filled life I thought, *Oh,
all I have to do is feel joy... and there, it's a joy filled life. That's all there
is!*

Learn Some New Skills: It's a Secret

When I saw *The Secret* I didn't know what to want. Life had taken
me down this path and I was being told there was little to nothing I

could do. The blow to my ego, my lifestyle, and my physical body kept me focused on the misery of the situation. I was in pain all the time; body, mind, and spirit. My ability to do the work I loved was gone and I had been given a life sentence of debilitating symptoms and a seemingly insurmountable list of increased ailments I was told was my most certain future. No wonder I didn't want to live. I was at a point of grasping like a frantic swimmer drowning in frigid water. I was reaching for anything anyone else could tell me I may be capable of doing. I was hungry to be part of a team again. I was hungry to have my own slice of the pie, something that I commanded and excelled at. Instead, I was being slapped down and away from the table of opportunities I was familiar with. So when it came to asking what I wanted, I found myself asking, "What *could* I want?" I was trying to identify myself in this new situation and I couldn't. I couldn't find my way out of the void.

The movie showed cars and relationships and an assortment of other wantables. My mind drifted to the reality that everything I had strived for was gone. My awareness of the new version of Mia was just emerging. I loved the movie, but thought I couldn't identify anything I wanted, beyond wanting my old brains back. I needed to start someplace more basic and more safe. It had to be something that I had control over that no person nor experience could ever take away from me. I had concluded it wasn't safe for me to think of wanting the things I wanted before:

- ✔ Beautiful mansion with a sprawling green lawn leading to the lake, complete with private dock and amazing views of big water, rocks, mountains, and trees.
- ✔ Midnight blue convertible sports car with manual transmission.
- ✔ Loving romantic life partner to explore, learn and share the world with.

No one could take away my thoughts. I would want a joy-filled life. The joy could be hidden away in my mind, and as long as I controlled my thoughts I controlled the joy. Even if things go the way I was being told was my certain future, this was the one thing I had control over. This was the ultimate. Following the directions from the movie, I used my five senses and I came up with this simple statement. I tore off the corner of a sheet of paper and wrote my desire in terms my senses already related to:

I feel JOY when…
I *see* colorful flowers in the garden,
I *smell* the fragrant plants,
I *feel* the texture of leaves,
I *hear* the sounds of birds,
I *taste* the morning dew off the crisp green leaves.

Now I needed to put it someplace I would remember so I could refer to it often. I needed to read it, feel the feelings deeply, and move on with my day. My desk was a mess of paper piles. My calendar was a mess of sticky notes. I wanted to keep it with me all the time, and since I had a habit of resting my hands in the front pockets of my pants, I decided to place the note there.

I was determined to feel the joy, to live the joy, and nothing was going to stop me. I was dependent upon visual and auditory cues to get me through those days. I wrote the note out and tested it; reading it and feeling it. *Yes, that would work well.* Then, I folded it up and placed it into my front left pocket. Like clockwork I put my hands into my front pockets and found the folded piece of paper. I wondered what it was, pulled it out, unfolded it, saw the words and remembered, *Oh, yeah—I wrote that.* Then I would remember I was supposed to read it and really feel it. Focusing on the words and the senses, I lived the feeling of *joy*. A few weeks went by and I determined it was true: focusing on joy did bring me more joy. I thought this was the extent of it. I went about living my life and following my interests.

What I hadn't recognized at the time was that those things I wanted before were actually coming true even before I saw *The Secret*. In the months previous I had moved to a beautiful mansion, but I hadn't recognized it because it was up on the hill overlooking the bay, not on the shores of the lake, and because I was renting it, not buying it. The sports car and the romantic partner came—and went—after I started practicing the new sensory skills I learned from the movie.

One Beautiful Mansion

I needed to move from the cramped, one bedroom, 500 square foot shack with a big yard that was home to me and my children. They were growing, the house was shrinking, and I needed more time and space to sequester and to calm myself. I asked my sister to help me find a place the kids and I could live comfortably and within my budget. The brain injury was taxing and my ability to make good choices was diminished. I no longer trusted myself and needed to ask others for help in making even the smallest decisions. Moving is not a small decision, but I needed another pair of eyes I trusted to tell me their opinion of my idea.

I wanted a three-bedroom, two-bathroom home, preferably a mother-in-law type apartment so I wouldn't have to deal with too many people and their noise. We found three bedrooms with one bathroom. It had a breathtaking view of the lake and mountains, and I could do as much yard work as I wanted. It was over my allotted budget, but within my means. We moved in. It was novel to have our own bedrooms and with doors that actually shut. We moved around easily in the 1,100 square feet and often out into the yard. That first year I pulled a lot of weeds and connected to the earth. It felt healing to be amongst the plants and the dirt. I used the backdrop of the garden to create my senses-based joy list.

A Midnight Blue Convertible Sports Car

Since I was feeling more joy—because I was focused on it—I decided, *Why not want a sports car?* The guy in *The Secret* provided great mental imagery and so I tried that one on as well. At first it seemed materialistic and perhaps not important enough to want such a thing, but I hadn't yet gotten the Corvette I had wanted since I was 17. This time, though, I wasn't looking specifically for a Corvette. I was thinking midnight blue, manual transmission, convertible. I put my order out to the Universe and within one week I was looking at a convertible sports car, but it wasn't quite what I wanted; it was black. I waited.

By the second week I had the car I wanted on order, and a year later that car was my fun toy. I marveled at how just two weeks prior I didn't know how I was going to pay for it. Then, by the time the bill arrived for my new ride, I realized I had more than the price of the car. I hadn't noticed the check I had placed on my refrigerator until I needed to come up with the money.

A Loving Romantic Partner to Explore, Learn, and Share the World With

My confidence for getting what I wanted started increasing and I put in my order for my tall, dark, and handsome romantic partner. I started envisioning us smiling and laughing and getting into my sports car. He showed up soon after.

Deepening My Reason to Believe

Watching both *What the #$*! Do We Know!?* and *The Secret*, I could see the correlation between feeling, thinking, and behaving, and was introduced to the idea of abundant possibilities that exist in every moment. I watched both movies multiple times as the ideas I found in them fascinated me. I learned about the science of the brain as it relates to function and experience. I embedded the belief that these desires—and more—would come true.

I was trying new things and redefining success during this time. My joy level was increasing and I decided I wanted to lose the 50 pounds I had gained since the accident. My attempts at exercising it off were met with increased pain and long recovery periods. I was living with constant pain from head to toe with brief attempts to return to the athletic level I had been accustomed to before the injury. My blood pressure was high and the neurologist was questioning if I'd had any seizures. I learned that seizures have been known to occur up to five years after impact. I was still experiencing what I called internal tremors. I felt the tremors at my core, but none registered during the now annual neurological checkup. My short-term memory was still collapsing on me and I had tried the medication the doctor prescribed. Nothing worked. I asked to be taken off the medications. On the third attempt and with awful side effects I was successfully weaned off. I was sleeping long hours, having challenges with daily living tasks, yet manifesting through it all.

A friend who knew I was trying to lose weight told me about the Master Cleanse, a fast where nothing is ingested but a concoction of water, lemon juice, some sweetener, and cayenne pepper. I had the habit of eating—I *loved* to eat. I enjoyed the short respite from pain the distraction would bring. But the Master Cleanse was liquid for days on end. I lasted about six hours, not the weeks I would need to sustain to remove the weight! Determined, I went to the website to figure out how I was going to pull this off. Once there my eyes locked onto a picture containing a bunch of pasty-skinned folks with one woman sporting a radiant, beautiful complexion. She looked beyond fabulous! She almost *glowed* with an aura I was drawn to. Upon reading further, the man who was touting the Master Cleanse said that was his wife and she was 'raw vegan' about six months out of the year.

The website had a link to a book: *The Raw Family* by Victoria Boutenko. I went to my library and checked it out. I read how this family of four had different health challenges; asthma, diabetes, obesity, hypertension, and more. According to the book, they 'went raw' and no longer experienced these issues. My mind began to ponder and I checked out all the books I could on the topic at the local library. Other books had similar and varied stories about people removing all kinds of maladies by eating this way. I read stories of how people who were overweight lost weight, but people who were underweight gained weight. There were the reports of people who cleared away various cancers, multiple sclerosis, brain tumors, Parkinson's disease, dementia, and a host of other ailments. I looked for the people with brain injury and found none, but I had found others with some of the symptoms I was experiencing: chronic fatigue, depression, obesity, hypertension, headaches, brain fog, body aches, and pain.

I decided to become my own experiment and see what would happen. From everything I had read, even if the debilitating symptoms of my brain injury remained, the side effect was going to be weight loss. I decided if that was as good as it got I could accept it. I was going to go full raw vegan overnight and see what would happen. I gave myself two months to prepare. I purchased a Vitamix blender, a dehydrator, and a food processor and started gathering recipes and ingredients. In anticipation I began to wonder how much of my brain power I could get back. Would I be able to be there more for my children? Could I return to my beloved computer job?

I began my experiment with a mind open to observation. Within three days I was feeling total bliss. I was standing in my kitchen eating an orange bell pepper when I began to notice something I can best describe as a vibrating sensation. It was getting faster and my attention followed it, then it suddenly seemed to 'pop' and I was filled with joy! I marveled at the sensation and realized, *Wait a minute, I was supposed to be depressed for the rest of my life!*

By day seven I realized the continuous aches and the unrelenting ice pick headaches were gone! Over the next weeks and months they were an occasional visitor instead of my constant companion.

During the fifth month a horrific headache captured me and I began to cry out. Holding my head with my hands I thought I was going to die. Then as suddenly as it started it released, and with that release a flood of words I had learned in college became accessible. In the days that followed I became aware of my newfound ability to automatically translate cooked recipes to raw versions and I began to create.

By the seventh month I had removed over 64 pounds of weight and toxicity; I was 14 pounds lighter than my weight at the time of injury and I felt fantastic.

It took 18 months to reduce the amount of sleep from 14-20 hours per day down to 10-14 hours. Naps were still sporadic and mandatory. Neurological overwhelm was still present but I was in awe of my ability to think in dimensions. I had gone so long without the ability to think. And my complexion was radiant.

I started to really believe anything was possible. Annual checkups with my neurologist continued to show my inability to return to regular employment, but I felt better and started to look for options to make contributions to society that fit my particular needs.

Years later, the dissolution of a romantic relationship brought struggles and I caved in upon myself. I started eating cooked food and then junky processed food. My mental faculties took a nose dive. Headaches became more frequent and a new level of depression set in. My mother invited me to visit her on the other side of the state, and while I resisted, it seemed like the Universe was directing me there. I complained. I didn't want to go there. I had determined that area was the armpit of America and I couldn't figure out why anyone would want to live there.

Identifying a New Dream

Reluctantly, I moved. I clung to disappointment and disbelief; I had pictured my life on a grander scale and in 'nicer' surroundings. I couldn't see the beauty that was all around me. I pondered, *Why this place?* Then I found out. This new location had a huge support group for people living with brain injury and the local community college provided one aspect of rehabilitation that I didn't receive in my early years of recovery. Ironically the class was called *Moving On.* I met many amazing people who, like me, suddenly found themselves thrown into the world of brain injury and all the *gifts*—which some call limitations and some call challenges—that go with it.

No matter what our ability, there is a place for each of us. Many people struggle with finding their place, especially after traumatic events where everything changes, and we are left to pick up the pieces and make peace with it all. It starts with identifying a goal and taking the steps to move toward it. I identified my goal standing in line to sign up for the rehab class. I was third in line with several others behind me. I was hearing the young man at the front of the line explain why his application was not filled out. He couldn't see the words on the pages and he didn't have money to go to the eye doctor nor to purchase glasses.

Just then my attention was directed to the heavy creak of the door opening and I turned to watch a man in his 40s walking into the building. He was pushing the door open with one hand and reaching into his mouth with the other. Then, pulling an object from his mouth, he looked at it closely before shoving it into the front pocket of his jeans. I would find out later it was his tooth. He didn't have money to go to a dentist.

In class I met a young man who had been a successful car salesman just a few months before, commanding a large income, who now couldn't afford the cognitive therapy that would make the difference between his one-word frustration and the satisfaction of a complete, cohesive sentence. Many among me are pros at going without. Some people go without everyday things the rest of us take for granted such as light bulbs and toiletries. Some stop dreaming, uncertain of what they can really accomplish now. Some stop reaching and succumb to despair. Others have stopped living, and instead turn to focus on existing within the bounds of a society that tells us we *can't* and describes us in terms of lack of ability, value, and worth; our minds soured and believing the programming of *another's* definition for our lives.

One day in class I was complaining about my life, where I lived, and what had become of me. "I'm 50 years old and I live in a trailer park!" I definitely wasn't living the life I thought I could; the life I deserved. I blamed my brain injury for holding me back and named it as the reason for my current situation. I was at a loss of how to get out of it, beyond suicide, and while I do experience suicidal thoughts from time to time, sometimes white knuckling it to get through the day, I was not interested in leaving that pain on my children nor on extended family members.

There are great teachers and there are teachers that change your life. Craig Sicilia was both. He was also the reason why the area I lived in was filled with TBI support groups. A TBI survivor himself, and one of the instructors in the Moving On class, he heard the pain behind my words. He turned to me and said, "*I challenge you to live a life better than the one you would have lived if you hadn't sustained brain injury*," and went on teaching the class without skipping a beat. That immediately derailed me from the negative track and my brain began chewing on this new challenge. I replaced the misery program with a solutions-based mental droid bent on solving the situation of how to deliver that *better life*.

That perspective stuck with me as I did the coursework. That quarter many things began to crystallize for me. I could identify interests; I identified my current strengths and weaknesses. We tackled topics like relationships, communication skills, good self-care, hobbies, work and volunteer interests, and dreaming new dreams as well as setting goals. We focused on building skills in those areas. We were dreaming in possibilities. I learned and continue to learn from my classmates. With the guidance of my instructors, Craig's challenge, and the supportive, cooperative atmosphere, I found my mission.

As it turns out, my mission is also tied to a declaration I wrote when I was 17 years old. In my youth I observed differences in the quality of peoples lives. The key was joy. I identified my desire to be a 'catalyst for joy.' The years passed and I had forgotten this desire. Then, after my accident and diagnosis 20 years later, in the depths of despair, I decided to live a joy-filled life. After meeting so many who are struggling like I did while coming to terms with their new ways of functioning I realized my mission:

To raise money for people living with disability (the individual, their family, caregivers) for their benefit to increase their quality of life. The monies I raise help people living with disabilities by providing needed medical services, enriching experiences, social opportunities, and coaching to assist them in identifying and reaching their goal, with the objective of learning to live a new dream and being supported in living it.

Refocusing My Mindset

I was involved with my first mastermind group while struggling to put together my money-raising website. I had several shifts during this time. We read a chapter a week of *We Were Born Rich* by Bob Proctor and met on Monday evenings for an hour over the internet and telephone to discuss, integrate the information, and learn from each other. This was very powerful and I began to eat up everything Bob had to share; in the book, on various websites, and through videos on YouTube. I was particularly interested when I heard him say something about success, particularly financial success, not having anything to do with smarts. I deduced that if financial success has more to do with habitual thought, then even a brain-injured person, who has great difficulty functioning at full capacity in mainstream America, could be financially successful. Once again I decided to be my own experiment. I decided to put it to the test and see how much money I could raise for my charities and how many lives could be improved.

I had been wanting to put together a particular kind of website. There was always some reason why it just never manifested, until during my time with this mastermind group, I decided it was something I *had to do*. I knew what I wanted. I didn't know how to make it happen. I got online and I was drawn to particular things that made it seem simple in those moments and eventually I completed it. I shared this with my mastermind group and also my story of brain injury to brain awakening. I spoke of what I found within the disabled community since I moved here, and what I'm doing about it. The group was inspired.

Ulrike Berzau, leader of the mastermind, suggested I write a book about my experience. The truth was I had already started the book-writing process three times, but had not completed any of them. I grabbed the latest version from my bookshelf and met with her. She was impressed and asked me if she could write a letter of introduction and send it and my manuscript to Bob Proctor.

Structure to Succeed

It had been years since I first signed up for Donna Kozik's course, *Write a Book in a Weekend*. As fate would have it, at the time I was ready to finish this book I received an email from Donna asking those of us alumni who had not published our book yet to join her in a special edition book writing weekend. I cleared my calendar and joined in. This process provided me structure, guidance, and support. I especially liked the challenges issued. It created an extra air of excitement and camaraderie as we encouraged each other through the process, asked questions of our fellow writers and contributed to each others success. I shared with my Facebook friends what I was doing and kept them updated as to how I was coming along during this process. *Everyone* was supportive. This was what I needed. This is what we all need to be our best, to live into our dreams and to move on and live the highest quality of life possible.

After the mastermind, I started being coached in a group led by Ulrike. We studied the *Thinking into Results* Program by the Proctor Gallagher Institute. Working with an effective coach has made *all* the difference. I continue to receive support through coaching and mastermind group calls. I've made progress past the point the doctors said I would reach, living a higher quality of life than I had been led to believe I would with a brain injury. Being part of coaching and mastermind groups takes the focus off the brain injury and makes me feel like a regular person who just happens to have some challenges. Everyone has challenges.

Human potential is an exciting topic for me and with continuous study it is one that brings greater understanding and delight.

Chapter Eleven

Habit Four: Leveraging Habits

We all start where we are and build from there. My motivation to live a joy-filled life reached deep to my core and opened me to possibilities I had not seen before.

Definition: Habit

A habit is an established behavior. Thoughts are habitual. Events occur in our lives and we assign meaning to them. What we feel about something will dictate our thoughts and we will base our actions on those thoughts. Directing and focusing on one's feelings is the key to controlling our experience.

It is as simple as the way we think. You know it's a habit when it's your go-to behavior, whether it's a thought (I'm a go-getter), a feeling (joy), or a physical manifestation (drinking a green smoothie every morning), it happens over and over again. It's visible in the personalities and behaviors of people with whom we surround ourselves. It's woven into the physical environment we observe.

Some examples of habits include:

- Attributes of Type A personality (high energy, driven, go-getter)
- Attributes of Type B personality (calm, quiet, self-reflective)
- Feelings; angry, happy, content, joyful
- Putting my hands in my front pockets
- Wiping water from public bathroom counter tops after washing my hands
- Eating (food quality/nutritive-mineral value)

At the fundamental level, the difference between a person with a habit of anger and a person with the habit of joy is simply in which emotion each person focuses more of their time and energy. This focus shapes our perceptions, causing us to notice more of one thing than another. In a reality where everything is present at all times, the simple act of directing your focus makes your experience of that point of interest grow.

I know many people who have the habit of joy. They focus on silver linings and what they can learn from a situation rather than the supposed mishap. They look for the good in everything. There is a vibrancy to interactions with people of the joyful persuasion. They are the ones that have an aura of awe around them. They are the people I like to be around just because it feels so good.

I've also known several people with a habit of anger. They stay focused on their perceived misfortune, fixed in tumultuous situations and rageful confrontations. Interactions with people of the anger persuasion are accompanied by a feeling of heaviness and chaos and being dragged down. Over time my happy attitude gives way to the strain and I begin to notice depressive thoughts like a virus overtaking my mind. It's as if my energy level lowers to match theirs or the situation.

There have been times when I have been the negative person, mindlessly dragging down those around me. The accident and injury provided many hours of feeling anger. Several years after the injury I came to realize feeling anger is simply a habitual behavior. Understanding this, I could let it go and trade it out for the habit of feeling joy. I consider habits of feeling on par with physical habits such as wiping up excess water from public bathroom counters, a habit I practice and observe of other women in public restrooms. It's as automatic as driving the same way to work, school, or the store. When our awareness of our thoughts, feelings, and actions is brought to the present moment, we gain clarity and the ability to change them.

Definition: Leveraging a Habit

A habit is an established behavior. Leveraging a habit means strategically stacking a new action or behavior on top of an already established one, creating results that can be measured in exponential terms and quantum leaps. Ultimately I leveraged my habits of breathing, focused feeling, and eating to create a whole new life.

Breathing

I was experiencing great distress and needed to calm myself. Most of the time this looked from the outside like me walking away and sequestering myself in a quiet, darkened room. Sometimes I couldn't get myself to the room before my rage spiked. I began the habit of taking a slow, deep breath as I walked through doorways. Another practice I started was envisioning a light switch in the *off* position when my energy or mood was low. I would flip the mental light switch into the *on* position and begin to feel my energy or mood increase. These practices were very helpful in shifting my state.

Focused Feeling

I started with my pocket mantra—my note to myself to remind me to feel the joy—by leveraging the simple habit of putting my hands in my front pockets. I was able to do this even though my memory would not let me recall I had written the note. Tactile stimulation of my fingers on the piece of paper in my pocket didn't remind me. It wasn't until I opened the folded paper and saw the words that I remembered I was the one who wrote it. Then it registered what I was to do: read the words with as much feeling as I could muster and to *really* sensate into that feeling of joy.

Eating

While I was studying the science of changing one's brain, my focus was on thoughts and controlling them, forcing them away from my painful experience. I noticed when I changed my diet away from things that aggravated my body, I was filled with bliss. I became (mostly) pain-free and my brain function increased. This was a sharp contrast to my experience just days and weeks beforehand. I marveled at the quick shift in my quality of life simply by changing what I ate. I decided this meant *raw vegan* was the way to go and thought it was the reason for my new, beautiful life. After many years I now attribute the change to the structure of my beliefs, feelings, thoughts, and actions which started with that simple desire to live in joy.

I have found using highly mineralized food as fuel to be very important to my mind and body's ability to function at higher levels. When I eat this way I feel more connected. A stark contrast to the feeling of disconnection, a feeling many others with brain injury can relate to. When I find myself eating less mineral-rich meals I detach again from high-level functioning and struggle to think through mud. My diet became the difference between laying on the couch all day, unable to function, and being out in the world, talking as fast as I do now, being able to think, and being a participating and productive member of society.

Before I changed what I was eating I had some tests done to see if I was allergic or sensitive to any foods. Test results showed sensitivities to wheat and dairy among other things. No wonder I didn't feel well after I ate anything with these ingredients in them. The raw vegan way of eating just happened to remove the antagonistic foods from my diet and gave me a new level of joy—even bliss—that I had not experienced before.

People Are Programmable Units

Over the years I've watched people, including myself, program themselves in and out of a variety of experiences. In my previous life in the tech-savvy world of corporate America my program was how I defined myself and was built into my personality. The program had relevance there. It fed my success loop in that environment but didn't translate with my new brain in the world outside that corporate structure. I had identified with those traits to such a degree that I came to believe these elements were who I was.

It took me many years of living with brain injury to realize that those behaviors I had used to define myself were simply habits; changeable units. As we travel through life we're constantly developing new habits and dropping old ones. Most people put themselves on autopilot and let the easiest actions around them lead them into developing habits, positive or negative, unaware they have a choice in the matter. Once you realize that the choice is yours, you can pick and choose habits, focusing on the ones you want and ignoring those you don't.

Even a person with traumatic brain injury can rewire their brain, as I did. Each of us can use what we already do to propel ourselves into living our dreams; building a staircase of new habits step by step. Perhaps we change the quality of the water we drink or the food we consume. It can be as simple as taking a deep, relaxed breath each time we walk through a doorway. The world is limitless. Our experience is self-propelled, ignited by our desires, fueled by our feelings and earned by each thought, deed, and action.

PART THREE

Recipes

"Eat the food you love that loves you back... and you will find the love of your life!"

When I started my raw food journey I decided to go all in. I wanted to see if this was something that would turn my life around. I wanted to be well. I wanted to play with my children again. I wanted to be there for them in a way I was struggling with. I wanted to remember things and I wanted to lose weight. Beyond that, I wanted to see how far this road could take me.

I came across one person who, when I was explaining raw vegan recipes, brushed me off with an air of competition as she boasted the simplicity she preferred: eating a pint of berries from the store or roadside stand. Some folks prefer a bucket of bananas, a bunch of romaine lettuce, a cucumber, avocado, or load of tomatoes. This is great and I respect that; I just like to play with my food. I enjoy the nuances of spices as they float over my tongue and the subtle hints of fresh herbs found in surprising places and in fun mixes. I am a foodie with a penchant for creating and I honor that just as I honor the simplicity and beauty of an avocado spooned out of its own peel. Okay, I'd still add some spices to it before it made its way into my mouth.

Occasionally I find people like the one above, but my health is not in competition with nor a threat to anyone else. I'm in it for my higher functioning that spills over to a higher quality of life. I desire to inspire others to live their best by simply sharing what I have experienced and what works for me, not to tell people how to live their life. I also don't tell people what is best for them. How would I know? I believe it is up to each of us to decide what that is for ourselves. I can provide some ideas of what was possible for me.

I can share with you how I prepare the food I enjoy and my experiences, but it's a journey and we each have our own path to travel. I always encourage people to go for what feeds their body, mind, and soul.

Definitions

I'm presenting these recipes in the light of raw vegan. This simply describes the boundaries imposed on ingredient type and the preparation methods. These definitions are very basic and are outlined here simply for the purpose of introducing you to the guidelines of the recipes.

Raw: Ingredients not heated above 118° Fahrenheit. Warming foods is accomplished by dehydrators and high speed blenders.

Vegan: No animal products.

When I tell people about raw vegan cuisine and introduce them to my recipes, I get many people who tell me they couldn't give up their meat, poultry, fish, etc. My response is always, *You don't have to.* I suggest you eat whatever makes your body feel its best. You don't have to be raw vegan to enjoy the recipes. They are universally tasty.

More quick and tasty recipes can be found at my website, www.SmartRawFood.com. All monies from purchases go directly to support my mission, which you can read more about at the end of this book and on my website.

Ingredients

I stopped consuming ingredients that agitated my system. I removed environmental toxins and ingredients my body was sensitive to. Minerals, vitamins, and essential amino acids can be found throughout the food kingdom, including plants. Many books will tell you what to eat; some of them even say why and describe what the foods do in the human system. Here I am sharing a few ingredients I used and had good results with. As ever, it is up to each person to determine what is best for them. Some medications negatively interact with certain food ingredients. Therefore, it is important to do your research and determine where substitutions would be in your best interest.

Legal disclaimer: It is important to consult a knowledgeable doctor about any changes in exercise or diet.

I look at the mineral content in what I eat, as well as amino acids and vitamins. I also consider how my body responds. At 16 years of age I recognized milk as something my body didn't want, and yet there are those who *insist* that it is good for me. It gives me mysterious rashes, eczema, boils, and earaches. And since I am the one who gets to experience either bliss or a stomachache, I trust my gut every time!

I am not going to discuss GMOs in this book. Genetically modified foods and plants produced via mutagenesis are discussed elsewhere.

Ingredients to Live By

When most people hear 'raw food,' they think of salad. While salads are a great staple, they're just the tip of the iceberg in the vibrant world of raw recipes. I'm sharing a few key ingredients, both common and unusual, and a few ideas for how to use them.

Blue-Green Algae

The edible varieties of blue-green algae, such as spirulina and those found in Klamath Lake, are rich in A, C, E, and B vitamins, as well as minerals such as calcium, magnesium and amino acids. They are also an excellent source of trace minerals such as iron, zinc, manganese, copper, and selenium. You can sneak blue-green algae into almost anything. Sprinkle it on salads; mix it into water, juice, or fruit smoothies; or blend it into Ocean Pâté or SuperHero Seduction (my famous chocolate sauce recipe) for an instant health boost!

Leafy Greens

Just like blue-green algae, leafy greens—kale, collards, and romaine to name a few—are packed with calcium, magnesium, iron, and amino acids, and rich in fiber and chlorophyll. Greens work well in many recipes: green smoothies, salads, wraps, and more.

Raw Nuts and Seeds (Walnuts, Chia, and Hemp)

There are many types of nuts and seeds with many different health benefits. I use cashews and walnuts in my Ocean Pâté recipe. Walnuts are good for the nervous system.

Chia is hydrating to the body. It's known for its ample antioxidants, fiber, and omega-3 fatty acids, and makes a great thickener in all kinds of recipes: smoothies, vanilla chia pudding, and even in vegetable-based tortilla wraps.

Hemp seeds are a rich source of protein, containing essential amino acids and fatty acids; omega-3s and 6s. Hemp also has high levels of antioxidants and help to enhance the immune system. Hemp seeds are great for sprinkling on salad or on desserts, in smoothies, and in Hemp Nog, a holiday classic!

Sea Vegetables (Irish Moss, Nori, and Kelp)

Seaweeds are rich in calcium, trace minerals, such as iodine, and contain phytochemicals—substances which are claimed to remove radioactive elements and heavy metals from the body. Irish moss, better known for its processed form, carrageenan, is a commonly used food thickener. Great for raw vegan lemon meringue pie and nut milk ice crème. Yum! Nori contains the highest amount of protein of all seaweeds as well as vitamins A, B1, and B3. Nori sheets make great wraps for Ocean Rolls, veggie rolls, or by themselves as a quick snack. Kelp is rich in fiber, potassium, iron, iodine, vitamin B6, and riboflavin. Kelp is great in soups and a key ingredient of my Ocean Pâté recipe.

Coconut

Coconut is another highly nutritious and versatile ingredient, high in fiber, protein, potassium, phosphorus, calcium, and trace minerals including magnesium, iron, sodium, manganese, zinc, copper, and selenium. I use coconut oil in my chocolate nut milk recipe as well as the Breakfast Shot recipe in this book. In addition to nutritional benefits, coconut oil's antibacterial, antiviral, and antifungal properties make it a great finish for bamboo cutting boards. I also use coconut oil on my skin as a moisturizer; applying it on wet skin after I step out of the bath or shower lets it soak in without leaving a greasy layer.

Cacao

Cacao can be processed into many forms including powder, nibs, paste, and butter, all of which come in handy in my recipes. Cacao is packed with antioxidants, fiber, protein, monounsaturated fats as well as B-complex vitamins and vitamin C and E. I use it in my Breakfast Shot, trail mixes, Seduction (my famous chocolate sauce), chocolate nut/seed milk, and smoothies!

Goji Berries

Goji berries contain all 18 amino acids along with megadoses of vitamin A, B1, B2, B6, C, and E, plus 21 trace minerals. Goji berries are rich in the unique phytonutrient antioxidants lutein and zeaxanthin, which are some of the most important nutrients for healthy eyes and nervous system. Goji berries are easy to snack on alone or in a trail mix, and great in medicinal goji berry tea or as a garnish for salads and other dishes. I love them in my raw chocolate bar (Raw Ecstasy) and my chocolate sauce recipes (SuperHero Seduction).

More About Ingredients

In recent years I've interviewed leaders in health and nutrition about mineral-rich, nutrient dense ingredients. I'm providing links to two of those information packed interviews here.

Brigitte Mars is an herbalist, nutritionist and author specializing in herbalism and natural lifestyle choices. I noticed that people with brain injury were often getting illnesses related to the endocrine system, so I asked Brigitte Mars about what people could eat to strengthen their endocrine system. You can view the video interview here: http://youtu.be/9qTHCWQOCkE

I interviewed Cherie Calbom, author of 25 books, speaker, retreat facilitator, and "juice lady" on my radio show. We talked about our experiences returning to health, the nutritional value of ingredients, and some of our favorite recipes:

http://www.blogtalkradio.com/braininjuryradio/2014/03/19/health y-living-with-mia-dalene

Equipment

These are a few gadgets that make food preparation fun, easy, quick, and tasty. The best gadget for you is the gadget you use.

The Basics: Knife and Cutting Surface

All kitchens should be equipped with a sharp knife and an appropriate cutting surface. My favorite are ceramic knives. They're lightweight, easy to handle, and the ceramic blade reduces oxidation~ resulting in your produce lasting longer after cutting. I also enjoy my bamboo cutting board, which I rub with coconut oil about every four to six months. *ceramic knives are used to cut fruits and vegetables. They are not useful in crushing garlic or cutting through bone. Twisting of the ceramic blade can lead to breakage.

High Speed Blender

My first love is the Vitamix, but I have since come to learn how to use the BlendTec. Both brands can be pricey, but well worth the investment. A budget-conscious option is David Wolfe's NutriBullet. Creaming nuts and seeds are easiest in the Vitamix and BlendTec. Any high-speed blender YOU love is going to work the best.

High-speed blenders have several uses, from soups, dressings, and sauces to grinding nuts into flour and creaming nuts and seeds for silky smooth texture, as I do for my signature Chi'Zcake, green pudding and smoothies, cashew cream, cashew-based Alfredo sauce, and Sunflower Pâté. My favorite use is for my Best Ever Jungle Peanut Parfait and other quick, high-mineral ice crème treats.

Food Processor

You can use this tool to cream nuts and seeds in a pinch, although they don't get as silky smooth as they do when using a high-speed blender. This gadget is useful in preparing nut- and vegetable-based chili, salsa, pâtés (Ocean Rolls, Mock Salmon Pâté), mango-lime-cilantro chutney, and the crust of my orange cacao tavolette. It can also be used to mince garlic quickly as well as to make *meit*, a spiced, crumbled walnut mixture that resembles ground beef, used in my Mexican dishes.

Dehydrator

You can think of a dehydrator as a 'raw oven' of sorts. It can be used for warming things up ~ like my vegetable lasagna, melting cacao and coconut butter as well as preparing raw pizza crust, tortillas, chips, crackers, fruit leather, coconut wraps, caramel coconut cookies and more.

Nut Milk Bag a.k.a. Mesh Bag

Definitely the cheapest gadget on the list and also one of the most versatile. Mesh bags are used to strain nut and seed milks and chi'Z and to grow sprouts. I use the pulp from my nut milks for cakes, brownies, crackers, croutons, and vegetable dip.

Spiralizer

A spiralizer usually comes with a collection of interchangeable blades that allow you to slice fruit and vegetables into stringy noodles or ribbons for sweet and savory meals or desserts. Some culinary delights you could make with this gadget include zucchini noodle alfredo or marinara, yam noodle Asian salad, and apple noodle tartlets with sweet cashew crème.

Juicer

There are two main types of juicer: masticating and centrifugal. Masticating juicers operate by crushing and squeezing the juice out of fruits and veggies, while centrifugal juicers shred and separate the juice and pulp afterwards. Both can provide nutrient dense fresh juice.

Masticating juicers can also be used to create pâtés of nuts, seeds, and vegetables which you can then dehydrate into nut loaf, burgers, and more. You can even make sorbets using fresh and frozen fruit!

Recipes

This is a sampling of recipes highlighting a variety of culinary delights. If you enjoy these or are curious of other culinary delights using nutrient dense, mineral rich recipes, visit www.SmartRawFood.com for even more. *Enjoy!*

dalene's Urban Trail Mix

The first year I created this recipe, I made it in bulk and gave it as gifts at Holiday time. It was a BIG hit with everyone on my list, ages 3 — 86!

Tools

- None!

Ingredients

- Seeds (pumpkin, sunflower)
- Nuts (pecans)
- Berries (mulberries and dark chocolate covered goji berries)

Preparation

- Combine ingredients using a ratio of 2:1:1 (Seeds:Nuts:Berries)
- Pack up and eat on the go!

PowerBoost Trail Mix

Tools

- None!

Ingredients

- 1 cup hemp seeds
- ½ cup goji berries
- ¼ cup cacao nibs (optional)

Preparation

- Mix and eat. Perfect for a snack on the go.
- NOTE: Take a little extra time and add cacao nibs for magnesium and antioxidants.

Medicinal Goji Berry Tea

Tools

- 1 quart glass Mason jar with tight fitting lid

Ingredients

- 1/2 cup goji berries
- 32 ounces pure (filtered) water

Preparation

- Place goji berries in Mason jar and fill with filtered water. Fasten lid and soak (in or out of refrigerator) for about five hours or overnight.
- When done soaking, pour liquid into a cup. Garnish with goji berries and fresh mint (optional).
- Serve warmed, at room temperature, or cooled.
- Refrigerate unused portion in tightly sealed glass jar. Keeps for several days.

SuperHero Breakfast Shot

Tools

- Shot glass (optional) or small mixing bowl

Ingredients

- 1 Tablespoon cacao powder
- ½ Tablespoon maca root powder
- ¼ Tablespoon cordyceps mushroom powder
- ¼ Tablespoon bluegreen algae
- 1 teaspoon hemp seeds
- 1 teaspoon coconut oil
- 1 teaspoon maple syrup or preferred sweetener

Preparation

- Place ingredients in bowl, mix, and eat.
- Optional: layer ingredients from bottom to top in a shot glass, mix, and eat.

Chop Suey

I created this recipe from childhood memories of times when our family tucked itself away in the booth of our favorite Chinese food restaurant. Rare and cherished moments when our busy mother was all ours! Yields one XX-Large or three medium servings.

Tools

- Large mixing bowl
- Small mixing bowl
- Knife
- 1 quart glass Mason jar with tight fitting lid

Ingredients

- 3 cups green cabbage, shredded thinly
- 1 cup red cabbage, shredded thinly
- 1 green onion, sliced
- 2 medium stalks celery, sliced diagonally
- 2-3 cups mung bean sprouts
- 1½ cup mushrooms, sliced
- 1 teaspoon ginger, minced
- 1 teaspoon garlic, minced
- 3 Tablespoons cold-pressed extra virgin olive oil
- 2 Tablespoons cold-pressed sesame oil

- ¼ teaspoon Celtic sea salt
- ¼ cup cashews

Preparation

Mushrooms

- Cut mushrooms into ¼ inch thick slices and place in glass mason jar.
- Add 1-2 Tablespoons olive oil and a pinch of Celtic sea salt.
- Fasten lid tightly and shake to coat mushrooms evenly. Set marinating mushrooms aside while you prepare the salad.

Salad

- Shred cabbage into thin noodle strips.
- Slice green onions.
- Dice celery.
- Combine sliced veggies with mung bean sprouts in large mixing bowl.
- To create the dressing, combine ginger, garlic, and oils in small mixing bowl. Stir or whisk to fuse flavors.
- Pour dressing mix over salad, add mushrooms and toss.
- Let sit for ten minutes, garnish with cashews and serve.

dalene's Ocean Pâté

Tools

- Glass container suitable for soaking
- Food processor with S-Blade
- Mixing bowl

Ingredients

- ½ cup cashews
- ½ cup walnuts
- 2 Tablespoons filtered or pure water
- juice of half a lemon (2-3 tablespoons)
- ½ teaspoon Celtic Sea Salt
- 1 teaspoon of kelp powder or granules* (*preferred)
- 3 Tablespoons onion, minced
- 2 Tablespoons parsley, minced
- 4 Tablespoons celery, finely diced

Preparation

- Place cashews and walnuts into soaking container. Soak for three to five hours. The pigment of the walnuts will bleed into the cashews, turning them purple and creating a "tuna" look to your pâté.

- Drain off soaking water from the nuts and rinse well.

- In food processor, combine nuts, Celtic sea salt, water, and half the lemon juice.

- With processor on, add the rest of the lemon juice slowly. This will provide a creamy texture. When complete, the mixture will have a smooth paste consistency.

- Transfer from food processor to mixing bowl. Add the rest of the ingredients—kelp, onion, parsley, and celery—and stir well.

- Roll mixture into a ball, place onto bed of spinach or romaine, and serve. Alternatively, can be served in nori rolls, a leafy lettuce or collard wrap, on a cracker, with some veggies as a dip, or eaten by the spoonful!

Cacao Mousse

Tools

- Glass container suitable for soaking
- Food processor
- Knife

Ingredients

- ½ cup dates, pits removed and soaked
- 1 medium to large avocado, peeled and pitted
- 4 Tablespoons agave nectar
- 1 teaspoon alcohol-free vanilla extract
- 2 pinches Celtic sea salt
- Water from soaked dates

Preparation

- Remove date pits and place in soaking container. Add water to cover. Soak for three hours or until soft.
- When dates are done soaking, drain water and set aside-keeping it to use later.
- Combine dates, avocado, agave, vanilla, and salt in food processor. Slowly add date water until smooth and light, or desired consistency.

- NOTE: As an alternative to using avocado, you may use Irish moss or young Thai coconut gel. Young Thai coconut water may be used as a substitute for both dates and date water.

Caffè Cacao

Tools

- High-speed blender

Ingredients

- 3 cups filtered water
- ½ cup cashews
- 2 Tablespoons cacao powder
- 1 Tablespoon coconut oil (or coconut butter)
- 1 teaspoon *Mucuna pruriens* a.k.a velvet bean (provides the coffee flavor)
- 3 Tablespoons agave nectar, or 1-2 pitted dates, or other sweetener of your choice.

Preparation

- Place all ingredients into high speed blender and process until smooth, creamy, and warm.
- Adjust ingredient ratios to taste.
- Serve warm, room temperature, or chilled from the refrigerator.

Red Pepper Bisque

Tools

- High-speed blender
- Knife

Ingredients

- 4 red bell peppers, seeds and stem removed
- 1 medium tomato
- ½ cup pine nuts
- 2 teaspoon coriander
- 1 garlic clove
- 2 Tablespoons lime juice
- 1½ teaspoon Celtic sea salt (start with one teaspoon and add more to taste)
- ½ teaspoon black pepper (start with the ¼ teaspoon and add more to taste)

Preparation

- Place all ingredients into blender and process until smooth and slightly warmed.
- Pour into decorative serving bowls, garnish with pine nuts and sliced basil and serve!

Green Pudding or Green Smoothie

Make sure your fruit is well blended before adding the leafy greens. This ensures you will not need to add water! You may choose to add chunks of fresh fruit, such as blueberries, apples, or mango to your bowl of green pudding for a burst of flavor and mouth-pleasing surprise. This can also be made into a smoothie by adding water to suit the consistency. Yields about 2 cups as pudding.

Tools

- High-speed blender

Ingredients

- 2 medium-sized apples of a sweet variety, cored and chunked
- 8-12 leaves dinosaur kale, stems removed
- 1 thick handful of Italian parsley
- ¾ Tablespoon blue-green algae
- chunks of fresh fruit; blueberries, apples, or mango (optional)

Preparation

- Place the apples into high speed blender and blend until smooth.
- Add kale and parsley leaves and blend again.

- Pour into serving bowl. Garnish with chunks of fresh fruit, sprinkle with blue-green algae, and serve.
- NOTE: Add more kale for a thicker pudding. Add water for a thinner smoothie.

Almond Flour

This recipe takes a while, so I like to prepare large amounts of almonds in advance and store them until I need them. This is a key component of dalene's Signature Chi'Zcake, but can be used for many recipes.

Tools

- Glass container suitable for soaking
- High-speed blender
- Food dehydrator

Ingredients

- Whole almonds
- Water

Preparation

- Place almonds in soaking container and fill with water. Soak for 24 hours.
- Drain soak water and rinse almonds well.
- Place whole almonds in dehydrator. Dehydrate for about 24 hours or until crispy.
- Place two cups of dehydrated almonds into high-speed blender and blend until they reach a powdery, flour consistency. It doesn't take very long. Repeat until you have the desired amount of flour.

- Store unused almonds in an airtight container in a cupboard or on the counter.
- NOTE: In hot climates, storing nuts and seeds unrefrigerated can cause them to go rancid. In this case you may wish to store them in the refrigerator.

dalene's Signature Chi'Zcake

Tools

- High-speed blender
- 9" pie pan

Ingredients

Crust

- 2 cups almonds, made into flour (see previous recipe)
- 1/8 teaspoon Celtic sea salt
- 1 Tablespoon olive oil
- 1 Tablespoon agave nectar

Filling

- 2 cups raw cashews, soaked 3-5 hours
- ¼ cup agave nectar
- ¼ cup lemon juice, fresh squeezed
- 3 Tablespoons coconut oil (or use 3-5 dates, unsoaked)
- 1 Teaspoon alcohol-free vanilla extract

Add For Chocolate Version

- 2 Tablespoons cacao powder

- 1 teaspoon cacao butter shavings

Preparation

Crust

- Place ground almonds and Celtic sea salt into pie pan, mix well.
- Add olive oil and agave nectar. When mixed well, and with the right amount of oil and agave, crust should pack well and crumble easily.
- Press into pie (or springform) pan.

Filling

- Place all ingredients into high-speed blender. Blend until creamy. Adjust flavors to suit your tastes.
- Pour into pie shell and place in refrigerator to set up, until pie can be cut and remain solid (about 20 minutes).

Tastes better with time, as flavors marry. Store unused portion covered in refrigerator. Will keep for two weeks or more.

Topping Ideas

For a gourmet finish, drizzle raw chocolate sauce (see next recipe) onto a clean plate in whatever pattern you wish. Place one slice of cheesecake on center of plate. Garnish with a sprig of mint and fresh raspberries. Alternatively, use slices of mango or lime.

Seduction

Mia's Famous Raw Chocolate Sauce. Yields about 1½ cups.

Tools

High-speed blender
Decorative jar (optional)

Ingredients

1¼ cup agave nectar
1 cup cacao powder
2 Tablespoons coconut oil
1 teaspoon alcohol-free vanilla extract

Preparation

- Place all ingredients into a high speed blender (liquid first so powder doesn't get caked under the blades) and process until creamy smooth. When blended properly, there should be a distinctive sheen to the mixture's surface.
- Taste, adjust ingredients as needed and mix well.
- Drizzle under your Chi'Zcake, over fruit or ice crème, or just eat by the spoonful!

This recipe does NOT need to be refrigerated even after opening. Theoretically, it could last over four months. Unfortunately I've never been able to test the theory as it always seems to disappear into my mouth long before that.

NOTE: When I teach this recipe, I encourage my students to make it, put it in special jars, and attach their own homemade label. This is a gift that is thoughtful as well as tastefully done! It makes a great gift for any gathering or as a way to say "thank you" to a special someone… especially if that someone is YOU!

SuperHero Seduction

Tools

- High-speed blender
- Decorative jar (optional)

Ingredients

1 batch of Seduction (see previous recipe)

Superhero Spice Mix

- ¼ cup cacao nibs
- ¾ Tablespoon maca root powder
- ¾ teaspoon blue-green algae
- ¼ teaspoon cordyceps (medicinal Chinese longevity mushroom) powder
- 1/8 teaspoon ginseng powder (optional)
- goji berries, to taste (optional)

Preparation

- Place all ingredients except cacao nibs into high speed blender. Blend until creamy smooth. *NOTE: You may choose to add the SuperHero Spice Mix to an already existing jar of Seduction, in which case, you may simply add dry ingredients and mix by hand.*

- Add cacao nibs and mix on low briefly to combine evenly throughout mixture.

- Adjust ingredients to taste.

- Pour out into decorative jars (or ½ pint Mason jars as I do), add your own label, affix tag that includes this recipe and give generously to everyone!

My Mission

How $12 Turned the Light on in 30 People's Lives

My intention to help others spurred me to create a survey to find out what my disabled peers thought and wanted. I wanted to help them reach their dreams so I needed to know what those dreams were. Among the questions I asked were the following:

- What is the nature of your disability, what is it, and how did you get it? There are many ways to receive a brain injury.
- What do you want others to know about you?
- What, if you had it, would increase your quality of life?
- Do you have any goals or things you would like to have or do, people you'd like to meet, or places you would like to go?

The toughest question to answer was the fourth question on goals and dreams. It was unanimous. Thirty students sitting in that classroom had left their dreams behind. They existed within the realm of what society was telling them they could and could not be and could and could not have. Figuring out what they were going to eat that day and if they could afford it had become more important than the art of dreaming, let alone dreaming big.

I read through the survey results with great interest. As a trained anthropologist, I was looking for patterns. They wanted what everyone wants. They wanted people to know they don't like being called derogatory names. They wanted to be treated with respect. They wanted to be included. They wanted to find love and live peaceful lives.

I was really interested in what they thought would increase the quality of their lives. The answers ranged from lightbulbs to train rides through several states to visit family. The big shocker to me was no one mentioned money as the thing that would improve the quality of their life. I was touched and inspired by their answers, and the thing that touched me the deepest was the simplicity of their requests. I shared the survey results with a handful of non-disabled folks. Each one touched in the same way I had been. And then there was Doris's answer.

Doris is a special person to me. She is kind, soft-hearted, considerate, thoughtful, and quiet. She takes notes in each class and keeps them organized in a green three-ring binder. She showed me two years' worth of class notes and offered to let me read any of them if I miss a class or if I just want to know what they talked about that day.

Doris identified lightbulbs and a case to put her yarn in as the things that would increase her quality of life. One of the people I read this to spoke up, "I can do that!" And by the time the group met the next week I had my first donation in hand and was presenting it to Doris. I stood at the front of the class and got everyone's attention. My short speech included a reminder of the surveys everyone filled out. Heads nodded. I spoke about the survey results and how we had our first donation. I held the package behind my back and asked Doris to come to the front of the room. She came up and as she realized what she was getting, she thanked me. Tears filled her eyes. We hugged.

I looked out over the class, now silent, and I said, "This means people listen to us when we tell them what we want." There was an eruption of cheers and clapping as we all realized in that instant people were listening and they wanted to help. New opportunities were born. Doris walked, a little bolder, back to her seat clutching her mega-pack of lightbulbs. Other students sat a little taller in their chairs. Our class started and I was hooked on helping people, realizing how easy it truly is to make a huge difference in someone else's life. It healed a portion of me and still resonates within me, driving me forward. This simplistic act feeds my soul at such a deep level. It is my passion and my mission.

So many things stop after brain injury. I choose to show the world how to keep on living. Not only living, but how to live a life greater than the one they would have had if they didn't experience brain injury. This is the life I live now.

A Word About My Mission

I am using my experience to create a better world.

All monies collected from this endeavor go toward the charity I am creating to benefit people living with brain injury. On my website, www.PhenomenalBrainPower.com, I share my vision and mission to raise money for people living with brain injury, to provide access to programs designed to help them with several things I observed as key to living a higher quality of life. These include;

- Assistance with medical services (cognitive therapy, dental, vision, and hearing).
- Social activities (social programs, vacations, seasonal camps, and social events).
- Educational opportunities that lead to identifying goals, learning to live a new dream, and the support needed for them to step into and live that dream fully.

As I explain on my website, these are things I observed in the disabled population as things we struggle with the most. It's amazing the new perspective that can be gained from having the proper eyeglasses, high quality hearing aids that actually work, and cognitive therapy that helps build new neural pathways. The isolation that seems built into the paradigm of living with disability can be offset with social opportunities like camping and seasonal vacations. Sharing these and other social and life experiences with others brings people out of isolation and into the world of living.

Charities That Fuel My Mission

Phenomenal Brain Power

www.PhenomenalBrainPower.com

www.SmartRawFood.com

Profits from purchases on these sites go toward medical services, social activities and educational opportunities for people living with brain injury.

People First – To Be Independent Support Network (TBISN)

a.k.a Traumatic Brain Injury Support Network

www.TBISN.org

email: Craig@TBISN.org

phone: (855) 473-3711 ext. 101

Monies donated to TBISN.org will benefit these programs:

4PEER11.org

The website to visit as well as the number to call (855-473-3711) to get brain injury peer-to-peer support by those whose lives have been affected by brain injury. You are not alone! www.4Peer11.org

BRAIN INJURY RADIO

Brain injury is a major cause of death and disability in the United States, contributing to about 30% of all injury deaths, yet it's largely unknown. Brain Injury Radio is a unique network of brain injury survivors who host shows every night with topics that can appeal to everyone. Listen live online and access archived shows at www.BrainInjuryRadio.com

Brain Injury Camp

A week-long camp out at North Skookum Lake in Washington state. This camp is designed for individuals and their families to relax, enjoy nature, and explore in the company of peers. Workshops, activities and discussions are presented by survivors, family members and special guests. Activities and campfire discussions encourage connection, learning, and fun. You can learn more at www.braininjury.camp

Brain Energy Support Team (BEST)

The Mission of BEST is to provide support, advocacy, public awareness, education, and socialization opportunities to individuals with a brain injury and their families. BEST distinguishes itself from other brain injury organizations in that the leadership, services, and programs are built by and for individuals with brain injury and their families. Check out their website to learn more about their Support Groups, Project PEER, Education & Outreach.

2607 Bridgeport Way, #2G
University Place, WA 98466
(877) 719-2378
www.BrainEnergySupportTeam.org

Brain Injury Resource Center

Providing a wealth of information, creative solutions and leadership on issues related to brain injury since 1985. "Services & Resources on this site reflect the best practices in the field of Traumatic Brain Injury."

www.HeadInjury.com
Brain@HeadInjury.com
Head Injury Hotline
(206) 621-8558

Resources

DVDs

- *Post Concussion* (1999) dir. Daniel Yoon
- *The Secret* (2006) dir. Drew Heriot
- *What the Bleep Do We Know!?* (2004) dirs. William Arntz, Betsy Chasse, Mark Vicente

Books

- *Choosing Joy in the Midst of Chaos* by Dolly Mae
- *We Are Born Rich* by Bob Proctor
- *Thinking into Results* by Proctor Gallagher Institute

People

Patricia K. Youngman, Speech/Language Pathologist
Best CogniCare - Cognitive/Communication Therapy
pkyoungman@gmail.com
206-619-2263
1401 Marvin Rd NE
Suite 307-262
Lacey, WA 98516

Constance Miller

Constance was my first knowledgeable contact with people who could help me. She is a wealth of information and an interesting person to talk with. It was at one of her workshops I began to learn about traumatic brain injury. This is also where I met my attorney, Fred P. Langer, RN, Esq.

www.HeadInjury.com
Head Injury Hotline
(206) 621-8558
Brain@HeadInjury.com

Fred P. Langer, RN, Esq.

NBLE Law/Nelson, Blair, Langer, Engle PLLC
1015 NE 113th St
Seattle, WA
(206) 623-7520

Gail Tumlinson & Craig Sicilia (Instructors)

Class: Moving On
Spokane Falls Community College
Spokane, WA

Bob Proctor

Proctor Gallagher Institute
www.proctorgallagherinstitute.com

Ulrike Berzau

Amazing Results
www.amazingresults4you.com

Donna Kozik

Write a Book in a Weekend
www.writewithdonna.com

Made in the USA
Columbia, SC
26 November 2017